William St. Chad Boscawen

From Under the Dust of Ages

A series of six lectures on the history and antiquities of Assyria and Babylonia

William St. Chad Boscawen

From Under the Dust of Ages
A series of six lectures on the history and antiquities of Assyria and Babylonia

ISBN/EAN: 9783337231736

Printed in Europe, USA, Canada, Australia, Japan

Cover: Foto ©ninafisch / pixelio.de

More available books at **www.hansebooks.com**

"From Under the Dust of Ages"

A SERIES OF SIX LECTURES

ON

THE HISTORY AND ANTIQUITIES

OF

ASSYRIA AND BABYLONIA,

DELIVERED AT

THE BRITISH MUSEUM,

BY

W. St. CHAD BOSCAWEN, F.R.Hist. Soc.

LONDON:

THE TEMPLE COMPANY, 6 Booksellers' Row, Strand, W.C.;

AND

SIMPKIN, MARSHALL & Co.

EDINBURGH AND GLASGOW: MENZIES & CO.

1886.

ILLUSTRATIONS.

CONTENTS.

——o——

THE CHALDEAN TEMPLE;

Its Construction and Services.

IF we would study the history of an ancient city, we must turn to its temple. The position which the temple occupied in the cities of ancient times was one of the highest importance. It was the germ, the heart of the city, and as the city and state grew in power, so the temple increased in wealth and magnificence; and when trouble and destruction fell upon the city, so were these adversities reflected in the annals, even in the very stones, of the temple itself.

The thorough explorations made by the late M. Mariette of the Temple of Karnak show, when Egypt was at the zenith of her power, how lavish were the offerings, how vast and rich the additions which the Pharaohs made to the shrine of their father, Amon-Ra; while its walls form, as Dr. Brugsch fitly remarks, a "history of the Theban kings." "No great cathedral or abbey," says Mr. Stuart Poole, "shows such a vast succession of labour, and so continuous a history. It is not alone a temple, but a library of historic records." So when the power of

A

the Theban kings waned, and the Ethiopian and the
Assyrian swept over the land, we see, in the
paucity of inscribed records on the walls, and the
meagre character of the halls and shrines erected,
the bruising of the reed of Egypt. In like manner
the temple of the Jews reflects the varied phases of
the nation's history. Less than half a century after
that most grand and solemn festival, by which the
Hebrew King Solomon had dedicated this dwelling,
rich with silver and gold and precious cedar, to the
Lord his God, in the days when "silver was as stones
in Jerusalem" (1 Kings x. 27), we find the Egyptian
spoiler Shishak carrying away to Thebes "the treasures of the House of the Lord" (1 Kings xiv. 25).
Rebellion and dissension had torn in twain that short-
lived empire, which for a time reached from the
Euphrates to the frontier of Egypt. Repaired by
succeeding kings, it is once more pillaged to furnish
the bribe to buy off Hazael (2 Kings xii. 18). The
Assyrian invasions of Sargon[1] and Sennacherib left
their mark on the temple (2 Kings xviii. 14, 15), and
its destruction was synchronous with the captivity
(2 Kings xxv. 8). Thus we see the history of the
Jewish nation reflected in the history of its temple.
The birth of a new city was marked in ancient times
by the building of a temple to the protecting god.
The origin of the custom is plainly to be seen in the
act of proprietorship in land. In the law tablet we

[1] See Sayce, "Fresh Light from the Monuments," pp. 117-118.

read—" For the future the Judge shall cause a shrine to be erected in a private demesne;"[1] so in like manner was the foundation of the more extended and royal property marked by the erection of a temple.

In Egypt, we find Memphis owing its origin to the foundation of the "House of the worship of Patah," and Thebes to that of Father Amon. We may, I think, see a somewhat similar recognition of the importance of the temple, not only to the religious, but also to the secular life of the people, prompting David, after the capture of the fortress of Zion from the Jebusites (2 Sam. v. 6-9), to remove the ark of the covenant, the Hebrew *palladium*, thither, and his wish to build in his new capital a house of the Lord (2 Sam. vii. 1). Turning now to Chaldea, we find the strongest evidences of the all-important position of the temple in the life and history of the city as in surrounding lands. The land of Chaldea was a land of temples; each city had its central fane, "the resting-place" of the patron god; while some of the more important cities, such as Babylon, Borsippa, and Sippara, had many of these sacred edifices.

The following is a list of some of the most important cities with their temples :—

---

[1] Probably to hold the *Kudurru* or boundary stone, on which the deed of proprietorship was written.

	City.	Temple.	Meaning.	God.
1.	Babylon.	E. Sagilli.	House of the Lofty Head.	Bel. Mero-dach.
2.	Borsippa.	E. Zida.	House of Life.	Nebo.
3.	Erech.	E. Anna.	House of Heaven.	Istar Nana.
4.	Sippara.	E. Parra.	House of Light.	Shamas.
5.	Ur.	E. Gir-nu-gal.	House of Sceptre.	Sin.
6.	Kutha.	E. Tig-abba.	House of Bowing down of the Head.	Nergal.
7.	Larsa.	E. Parra.	House of Light.	Shamas.
8.	Sergul.	E. Ser-gulla.	House of the Great Flame.	Fire God.
9.	Nipur.	E. En. gi.	House of Bel.	Bel.
10.	Nineveh.	Bit. Kit muri.	House of Love.	Istar.

Although we may regard the temple as a most important religious structure, yet we cannot, as I shall show, consider it as the first. The rude altar of a few hastily gathered stones, with the Akkadian and Semetic nomads, as with the Hebrew patriarchs, long preceded the temple; and it was not until the nomadic life was abandoned that the temple as the "House of the God" was built. Possibly intermediate between the two was the sacred enclosure, the *temenos*, in which the altar stood. This seems to be in some degree implied by some references in ancient Akkadian hymns to the enclosure of Eridhu. The importance attached to the right construction of altars among the early Vedic Aryans is shown by Dr Haug, in a paper read before the London Con-

gress of Orientalists, to have originated their first
ideas of geometry. The construction of the Chaldean
temple is based essentially on that of the house—it
being *E-Dingira*, the "House of God" of the
Akkadians, the *Bit-ilu* of the Shemites. That its
plan and ornamentation were settled at an early
period, and adhered to throughout with the strictest
of priestly conservatism, is demonstrated by comparing the plans of temples, which the spade of the
explorer has brought to light, with the original plan
drawn by a Chaldean architect more than forty centuries ago. This important design is now preserved
in the Louvre, where it forms one of the most precious treasures of the Assyrian Department. In
1879, M. de Sarzec, the French Consul at Bussorah,
undertook, on behalf of the French Government, a
series of explorations in Southern Chaldea. During
his travels in those regions in 1875, his attention
had been called to a mound situated about twelve
miles south-east of the ruins of Warka, the site of
the ancient city of Uruki, the Erech of Genesis, the
ancient capital of Chaldea.

The explorations resulted in the recovery of a collection of antiquities, monuments, and inscriptions,
which form the most valuable portion of the Assyrian
treasures of the Louvre. The chief edifices below the
ruins of Tel-Lo were a large temple and palace of
simple but massive construction. The only decoration was a series of buttresses at equal distances

along the walls, and double buttresses flanking the
doorways, similar in style to the ornamentation of
the buildings found at Mughier and Warka by Mr
Loftus, and by Mr Rassam at Aboo Hubba. In the
centre of the ruins was found the statue of the ruler
or viceroy who restored the temple, dedicating important gifts to it, and regulating the sacrifices and
offerings. This statue is a marvel of antique work,
such as Egypt only had hitherto produced. The
figure is about 4 feet high, and represents the ruler
Gudea, who bears the title of Viceroy of Sergulla, he
being an official under Urbahu, the ruler of Erech.
Gudea appears here in his character of chief architect of the temple, like Semnut, the royal architect
of the Egyptian Queen Hatasu, that profession being
in high repute in Chaldea as in Egypt. He is clad
in a long robe reaching to the ankles, and seated on
a throne without a back. The hands are folded in a
manner peculiar to Chaldean and Assyrian art, and
on the knees is a stone tablet, on which is drawn a
plan of the temple in which the statue was found.
This plan shows a building with buttressed walls and
doorways similar to the edifice uncovered by the
explorer. The date of this statue cannot be placed
later than B.C. 2120; and, judging by comparison
with other monuments and inscriptions, it may, with
a fair degree of accuracy, be placed about B.C. 2500.
It is evident, from the comparison of this early
specimen of the draughtsman's art, that Babylonian

sacred architecture became stereotyped—at least in plan—at a very early period, as we find the temples discovered by Mr Rassam at Aboo Hubba, at Balla- wat and Nimroud, present but slight variation from this ancient plan. That the construction of the ancient buildings, even at the remote period of twenty-five centuries before the Christian era, was a matter of care and mathematical calculation, is proved by this plan of the temple at Sergulla. Upon the side of the tablet, near the right hand of the sacred architect, is the burr or graver with which the plan was supposed to be drawn, and upon the front edge of the tablet is a neatly constructed and sub-divided scale, which, according to the accurate measurements made by Mr Flinders Petrie, gives a cubit of $20\frac{3}{10}$ inches, corresponding to the cubit of the old Empire of Egypt.

The explorations carried out by Mr Rassam at Aboo Hubba have restored to us the remains of a temple, which Chaldean tradition had always regarded as the most ancient in the land. According to the statements of Berossus, it was in the temple of the Sun god, in the city of Sippara of the Sun, the Chaldean Heliopolis, that Xisuthrus, the Chaldean Noah, buried the records which, by order of the god Cronos, he had written of ante-deluvian times. The explorations which the able explorer has carried out in the mound of Aboo Hubba, situated on the Yussifieh Canal, about thirty miles south-west of Baghdad, have proved that here was the site of this ancient city of Sippara—the Sapharvaim of the Bible.

The citadel occupies the southern portion of the *encienté,* and its highest point on the south-west face was once on the banks either of the Euphrates itself, or of a broad canal communicating with the river, the channel of which is now marked by the Ruth-wanyieh Canal. The trenches excavated in the mound soon struck the walls of a building, and, by following the line of this wall, the outer face of a large square edifice was uncovered. The portions of the walls laid bare exhibited a style of architecture and ornamentation similar to the buildings discovered by Mr K. Loftus in the mounds at Mughier and Warka, and by M. de Sarzec at Tel-Lo—the walls being broken at equal distances by projecting but-tresses, and decorated with ploughed pannels. Trenches and shafts sunk in the interior showed that within this outer rampart, which in some cases was over 18 feet in thickness, there were over 100 chambers ranged round a central court. In the cen-tral portion of the mound, an important pair of chambers were found. Approached from a court-yard, a doorway gave entrance into a large chamber, 100 feet in length, and about 35 feet in width. In the centre of this chamber, the explorer found the remains of a large brick altar platform, about 30 feet square, upon which, from charred fragments about, it was evident that the altar of burnt-offering of the temple had stood. The axis of this chamber was north-east and south-west, and at the north-east end a doorway was found, leading into a smaller chamber, measuring 45 feet × 35 feet. The floor of this chamber was paved with a material resembling very closely in composition asphalte. Guided by his former researches' at Ballawat and Nimroud, Mr Rassam sank a shaft through this floor in search of foundation records, which were usually buried beneath the floor, and discovered by a terra cotta box containing three inscribed records—namely, a stone tablet with a sculptured pannel, representing the worship of the Sun god, and two inscribed barrel cylinders. The cylinders were found to bear inscriptions of Nabonidus, king of Babylon, B.C. 555, recording the restoration of this temple in the year B.C. 550, and the stone tablet bore a long and important record of the restoration of the temple by Nabu-abla-iddina, king of Babylon, whom we already know as a contemporary of Assurnazirpal and his son Shalmanesar III., kings of Assyria, and whose date may be given as about B.C. 852. It required but a casual examination of the inscriptions to ascertain the nature of the edifice which the explorers had entered, as on the tablet of Nabu-abla-iddina, above the figure of the Sun god, is the inscription—"The statue of the Sun god—the great lord—dwelling in E. Parra (the House of Light), which is within the city of Sippara." An examination of this pair of chambers showed them to be in very fair preservation, though all objects of value had been removed, including the statue of the Sun god, which had once stood in the smaller inner chamber. It was most fortunate that so good an example of the Babylonian temple should be thus discovered, and it was soon made all the more important when the inscriptions discovered in the record chest furnished such conclusive evidence of the great antiquity of this temple. In his cylinder inscription, Nabonidus records that in his pious search for the records of his ancestors, who in remote times had restored this temple, he found the cylinders of Naram-Sin, the son of Sargon, who had restored some portions of this edifice 2300 years before. This, therefore, gives to this edifice a foundation prior to the year 3750 B.C.

Additional confirmation of this date is now afforded by the repetition of the same date in a second copy of the same cylinder, and also by the fact that other dates of less remote antiquity in the inscription when compared with the existing canon of Kings, are found to be accurate. Still more important, however, is the discovery, in the lower strata of the temple area, of a small ovoid of pink and white marble, bearing an inscription of Sargon I., the father of Naram-Sin, which, from its archaic character, bears strong testimony to the accuracy of this date. We may therefore note that, although this date does not confirm the statement of Berossus as to the ante-deluvian origin of the ancient city and its temple, yet it does establish this great antiquity. I now pass to the subject of the plan and arrangement of the temple, and to explain the symbolism therein.

The temple was called by the Akkadians E-Din-gira, "the House of God;" by the Semetic Baby-lonians, Bit-ilu, ' the House of God"—the Beth-el of the Hebrews. Many other titles were applied to it, such as "Resting-place of the God," "Dwelling of the God," "Palace of the God," "High Place," &c. The primary idea of all was, however, that of the temple being the "House of God," just as the palace was "the great house;" and it requires very little inspection of the plan to see how slightly it differs from the pairs of dwelling chambers which are found in the court-yards of Assyrian palaces, as at Nimroud, or in the more secular parts of the temple. The outer and larger chamber, in which the altar stood, corresponds to the living room; while the smaller inner chamber may perhaps be compared with the chamber called the inner chamber, in 2 Kings x. 2, in the commoner class of house, and, as I shall show, to the Harem in the palace. In the cuneiform in-scriptions, and especially in the later Babylonian writings of the time of Nebuchadnezzar, we find the name *Ekallu*, "Palace" or "Great House"—the Hekal of the Hebrews often applied to the temple. As, for example, in the cylinder (W.A.I., Vol. V., pl. xxxiv., col. i., line 47), we find the great temple

of Merodach at Babylon called " The Palace of the
Heavens and the Earth, the abode of Justice."

The application of this word to the temple in the
Assyrian inscriptions is similar to its use in a general
sense in the Books of Kings and the Prophets, where
the temple at Jerusalem is called the *Hekal-Jehovah*,
"The Palace of Jehovah," though we do not find it
applied in the more special sense of the Naos, the
larger chamber of the temple. The cella, or inner
chamber, of the temple bore several names in the
inscriptions, all of which are of importance as throwing light on the ideas embodied in the construction
of the temple. The most common name was Parakku,
a word of Akkadian origin, borrowed by the Semetic
Babylonians. This word had gone through various
changes of meaning. Its primary meaning, on
analysis of the construction of the word, was Parakku, " High Altar," and indicates the stage of
religious development, of which I have already
spoken, when the altar was the chief religious construction. And as the altar was a sacred spot, only to
be approached by those who were properly qualified,
so at a later time we find it applied to the Harem
of the palace, as Sennacherib calls himself in his
inscription, "The first-born of the dwellers in the
Parraku—that is, in the Harem." The further application of the word to the Holy of Holies of the
temple embodies the same idea of the sacred character of it in relation to the house of God, as the

Harem was of the private house. Indeed, we may say that this word, in its various applications, has undergone almost similar modifications to those of the Arabic word *Harem*, meaning first a forbidden spot, either the altar or courts of a temple or mosque, and the women's quarter of a house. Two other names applied to this *cella*, or "Holy of Holies," in the Chaldean temple were Kua and Papakha. The words occur in many cases together as if two closely associated portions of the sacred edifice. As, for example, in the India House inscription of Nebuchadnezzar (col. ii., line 40)—"In E-Sagili, the palace (*E. Kal*) of his lordship in their beauty, the House of the Oracle (Kua) and shrine (Papakha) of the Lord of the gods, Merodach." And again in the same inscription (col. iii., line 36)—"The beams of the ceiling of the shrine of Nebo with gold I covered. The cedar planks of the gate of the Oracle (Kua) I covered with bright gold." Comparing these and other passages, we may probably consider the Kua to be the Oracle, equivalent to the Debr of the Jewish temple, while Papakha was the shrine of the god. The cedar wood doors, which divided the holy place from the Holy of Holies in the Chaldean temple, resemble the doors which Solomon made for the entrance to the Oracle—"For the entering of the Oracle he made doors of olive wood, and he carved them with carvings of cherubim and palm trees and open flowers, and overlaid them with gold" (1 Kings

vi. 31-32). The writer of the Book of Chronicles, however, replaces these doors by the vail (2 Chron. iii. 14). The *Parraku*, or cella, was the most richly decorated portion of the Chaldean temple, and, like the Holy of Holies of the Jewish temple, was often one mass of gold, silver, and precious stones. In the annals of many of the Babylonian kings, we find reference to their lavish decoration of this Holy of Holies of the great temple of Bel Merodach. Gold, silver, and cedar from Lebanon were used with most lavish hand, but the most detailed descriptions, though somewhat mutilated in the case of the former, are found in the inscriptions of Assur-bani-abla and Nebuchadnezzar. In a fragment of cylinder, the Assyrian king thus speaks of his restoration of the temple of *E-Sagili :*—" E-Sagili (the temple) of the lord of the gods I made. I completed its decorations. The mother Bilat, the protectoress, of Babylon. Hea and Shamas from the midst of the temple I brought. I caused them to enter into the city of Suanna (the sacred quarter of Babylon). Their noble shrine I adorned with fifty talents of bronze. I adorned ————; with bricks I finished and enlarged upon it. I caused a ceiling of cedar wood to be made beautiful as the stars of heaven, adorned with beaten gold. Over Merodach, the lord of the gods, I rejoiced my heart. I worshipped him, and performed his will. A noble chariot the carriage of Merodach, prince of the gods ; with silver, gold, and precious stones I finished its work. To Merodach, king of the hosts of heaven and earth, the sweeper away of my enemies, a couch of accacia wood, for the holy place adorned with precious stones, silver, and gold, as the resting-place of Bel and Bilat—givers of favour, makers of friendship, skilfully I made." Not only does this extract from the inscription furnish a very good idea of the magnificence of this great temple, but it also mentions two objects of interest which were stored in that edifice. The first is the sacred chariot of the god. Merodach, as the Divine warrior, as he is called here the "sweeper away of enemies," the opponent of evil, would certainly have his sacred chariot. In Egypt, and among the Greeks and Romans, sacred chariots were kept in the temples. In an inscription in the British Museum, mention is made of " sacrificial rams for the yoke of the chariot of the great Lord Merodach dwelling in E-Sagili." So that there seems to have been a similar idea of his chariot being drawn by rams, as that of Dionysius was drawn by panthers or tigers. The sacred couch here referred to is probably the same as mentioned by Herodotus as one on which those wishing to con- sult the oracles of Belus slept. The discovery in the temple of the Sun god at Aboo Hubba of the pre- cious records of the royal donors, enclosed in a sacred chest, and of the foundation records of the temple at Ballawat—found, too, in a chest—affords a close re- semblance to the placing of the ark, containing the most precious memorials of the Hebrew religion in the oracle of the temple at Jerusalem. The existence of the large altar of burnt-offering in the outer chamber would seem to indicate that this portion was not roofed—only the cella or *Parraku* being roofed.

The most important object, however, in the *Parraku* was the statue of the god in whose honour the temple was erected, which was enshrined within this most holy part of the temple, as the statues of the divinities of Greece were within the cella. Of statues which in ancient times had occupied the *Parraku* of Chaldean temples, it is doubtful if we have any authenticated example. The statues discovered by M. de Sarzec at Tel-Lo, and by Sir Henry Layard at Kileh-Shergat, and Nimroud, came from temples; but we cannot definitely state that they were the images of the gods in whose honour the temples were erected. Still, however, we are not without information regarding such statues. The inscriptions of Agu-kak-rimi, a Kassite king of Babylon ruling in about the 14th century B.C., and the tablet of Nabu-abla-iddina (B.C. 852), already referred to, furnish most detailed and valuable information regarding these sacred images. In the latter inscription, we have the account of the making of one of these sacred images, which the king dedicated to this temple of the Sun god in the city of Sippara, in gratitude of the aid that divinity had afforded him in defeating the invaders of the land. The

passages relating to this statue are as follows :—
" Nabu-abla-iddina, king of Babylon, for the making
of this statue, ordered and set his face. This
statue he saw, and (with) its front and back he was
pleased. For the making of this statue his mind
was set. By the wisdom of Hea, (and) by the aid of
the Lord of the Bright Eye, the Lord of Gold, &c.,
of bright alabaster, the statue of the Sun god, the
great lord firmly he made." In the presence of Hea
and Merodach, the presence of the Sun god in the
House of Alabaster, which is on the banks of the
Euphrates ; its surface he cleansed, and raised to its
seat. The statue is represented in the bas relief,
upon the upper part of the tablet, as a seated figure,
clad in a long striped robe, and remarkable for the
luxuriant hair and beard. Of the statues associated
with temples, those from Tel-Lo and Kileh-Shergat
are all seated, and it is evident that, in the early stages
of Babylonian art, with few exceptions, and these
mere rude blocks, the Babylonians never attempted
to represent the full upright figure in the round ; still
less did they venture on the reproduction of the nude.

Two things seem to have militated seriously against
the attainment of beauty in these temple statues, and
indeed in all Assyrian art. The first was the Semetic
prejudice against the study and representation of the
nude, which M. Perrot has remarked hindered Assyrian
art from ever shaking off that stiff, narrow, and
conventional style which characterises its work.

The second retarding element may be found in the custom, of which ample evidence is afforded in the inscriptions, of clothing the statues with robes, which rendered anatomical correctness of little importance, and converted these early examples of the sculptor's art into a series of lay figures. In the earlier inscription of the Kassite king, which I have mentioned, we have a number of the adornments of the images of the gods mentioned, such as blue robes, robes woven with gold, and gold " crowns of divinity " set with precious stones ; and, in the inscription of Nabu-abla-iddina, the king dedicates " six beautiful dresses, the portion of the year," for the use of the temple, in which the statue was placed. Among these robes we may notice " striped robes " (*Zubat Scria'tu*), evidently similar to the one in which the statue is represented ; (*Zubat Damka Kakabi*), a " beautiful starred robe," also "a robe of open work ; " (*Zubat Khullanu*) ; and other adornments. The seated statue placed in the ancient Chaldean temples was copied in slavish manner by the Assyrians, and by them transmitted to the Hittite or Prehellenic tribes in Asia Minor, as shown in the sculptures at Eyuk and the Niobe of Mt. Sisyphus ; and, as Mr Gladstone remarks, the only statue mentioned in the Iliad—that of Pallas Athene—must have been a seated one, as in no other way could the priestess Theano have placed the *peplos* of Hecuba on its knees (Iliad vi., 302, 303) ; and indeed this ceremony

ASSYRIAN IDOL FROM KHORSABAD.

of the Trojan women seems to indicate a similar custom of adorning the gods, being in use in Homeric times.

I now pass from the question of the construction of the temple to that of sacrifices and ceremonies which constituted its ritual, and here we find matter of the highest importance to the student of Hebrew and Phœnician customs.

It might naturally be expected that a religious system, whose temples were arranged with such care and attention to symbolism, would have formulated a definite and elaborate sacrificial code. In this we are not disappointed. The information which has been acquired from the inscriptions, and especially from the later discovered examples, throws great light upon the system of sacrifices in Chaldea. The earliest code known is one found engraved on one of the tablets from Tel-Lo, dating from about 2500 B.C., and it is a document of considerable interest, as it is evidently pre-Semetic in character. In that inscription we find only bread, fruit, wine (Sikkaru), fruits, and flour forming the offerings, reminding us, in their primitive character, of the sacrifices of Cain, the "tiller of the soil," in contradistinction to those of Abel, the "keeper of sheep."[1] No mention is made of any animal victims. The two inscriptions, however,

[1] This inscription has been published by Dr Jules Oppert in the Transactions of the International Congress of Orientalists at Berlin, and I read it as follows :—1 Ephak of Sikkaru drink, 1 Epah of Food (Bread), ½ Epah of Fruit, ½ Epah of Flour. Each day is measured out.

which give us the fullest particulars of the sacrifices are the tablet of Nabu-abla-iddina, from the temple of the Sun god at Sippara (W. A. I., Vol. V., pl. 60), and the Philips cylinder of Nebuchadnezzar (W. A. I., Vol. I., pl. 65). Taking the sacrifices in order, I shall treat first of the victims. These are—" The ox, sheep, and rams." As we read in the Sippara tablet (col. iv. 29-32)—" Victims, the offerings of the heart, of great oxen, rams, fine large white sheep, he offered." (col. v. 16, 17)—" Of the victims of oxen and rams of the offerings." Also in the Taylor cylinder of Sennacherib (W. A. I., Vol. I., pl. 37, line 60), we have the following record of the sacrifices appointed by Sennacherib after his victory over Merodach-Baladan—" One ox, ten rams, ten omers of wine, twenty omers of first-fruits, to the gods of Assyria, my lords, I appointed in rotation." The Sippara tablet gives the portions of the victims to be retained by the priests, the remainder being sacrificed to the gods—" The rump, the tail, the skin, and the flanks, together with choice portions of the stomach and intestines, were to go to the priests, leaving the head and shoulders, with certain portions of fat, for the sacrifices." Thus we find, as under the Levitical law, a definite portion was set apart out of each offering for the maintenance of the priests (Levit. vii. 28-34 ; Numb. xviii. 8-19), a like provision was made in the sacrificial codes of Carthage and Marseilles. From Sippara, we learn that two classes of sacrifices familiar to us from the Hebrew ritual were in use in Chaldea—"The offerings and peace-offerings of the temple E-Parra of every kind." The offerings we may take to be the ordinary burnt-offering, as in Levit. i. 2-14, here called *Karibi*, literally "an approachment." The peace-offering is called *Salma Kurubti*, and corresponds to the sacrifice ordered in Levit., chap. iii. It is evident, from the very emphatic expression already quoted as to the sheep offered in the temple, which I read *Zeni-Magaru Damkate Kabrute*—"Sheep pure, large, and well favoured"—that the victims under the Chaldean, as under the Hebrew law, were to be without blemish (Levit. i. 3, 10 ; iii. 1, 6). The heave-offering, which takes so prominent a part in the Hebrew code, was also in use in the temples of Chaldea, as we infer from two inscriptions in a religious tablet (W. A. I., Vol. IV., pl. 32)—"A victim he kills, raising 'it in the place of his god, worshipping," clearly points to the lifting up of the offering in the presence of the gods. Also in the calendar inscription (W. A. I., Vol. V., pl. 48), we have mention of "heaving or lifting up flesh before the statues." The passage I have already quoted speaks of "first-fruits" (*Suluppi Reseti*) ; and among the Egibi tablets from Babylon, and the contract and fiscal tablets from Sippara, are large numbers of receipts for the "first-fruit dues." Passing now to the meat and drink offerings, the above-mentioned cylinder of

Nebuchadnezzar contains very full information on these points—"The portion of the gods of E-Sagili and Babylon, to each a daily portion prepared. I apportioned honey, milk, beautiful butter, and bread made with oil ;[1] honey wine, sweet syrup drink, and noble wines." This extract, which is repeated with some variations in the text, is full of matter of interest. The offerings of honey, milk, and butter are peculiar, as all three are excluded from the Hebrew code, and honey is expressly forbidden (Levit. ii. 11). The *Karānuv Dispāv*, the " honey wine," is evidently the *Dibs* of the Hebrews, mentioned in Genesis (xliii. 11), as one of the components of the present taken by the children of Jacob into Egypt for Joseph, and also by Ezekiel as one of the objects imported by Palestine into Tyre (Ezek. xxvii. 17). Most commentators regard it as the same as the Arabic *Dibs* and the Italian *Musto Cotto*. An important distinction is made here between the *Sikar Sutu*, the *Sheker* or drink offering of the Hebrews, and the grape wines, which are enumerated. Among the latter, we may notice specially the wine of Khilbunu or Helbon, also mentioned by Ezekiel (Ezek. xxvii. 18). These various wines and liquors formed the drink offerings of Assyria, and we often see, as in the lion hunt, the king pouring out libations to his gods. Another offering, common alike to the Hebrew

---

[1] *Akul Samnar—* the only rendering I can suggest, *Samnar* being the Hebrew *Semen*, " oil " or " fat."

and the Chaldean, was the sin offering, as shown by
Mr Pinches in his translation of the Nabonidus
Chronicle. He has certainly obtained the right rendering in the phrase, "A sacrifice for sin they made,"
though its analysis is rather difficult (Trans. Soc.
Bib. Arch., Vol. VII., pp. 160-162). "A sacrifice
for sin, they made victims in E-Sagili and E-Zida,
to the gods over Babylon and Borsippa, for peace he
gave," In the Scriptures we often see loaves of
bread placed before the altar of the gods, or on small
temporary tripod altars. But perhaps we may find
a closer resemblance to the tables of shew bread in
the series of small altars which Mr Rassam found
ranged on either side of the central aisle of the
temple of Istar at Nimroud, one of which is now
exhibited in the Nimroud central saloon of the
British Museum. I will conclude this *résumé* of the
Chaldean sacrifices by a quotation from one of the
sacrificial litanies (W. A. I., Vol. IV., pl. 68). I may
mention here that the word rendered "offering" in
this text is *Kurban*, the Hebrew Corban, "a gift"
(Levit. i. 2, and Matth. vii. 11). The tablet is broken
at the commencement :—

After him (the priest) to Nusku in like manner thus he shall
        say—
" Oh, Nusku, renowned one, counsellor of the wisdom of the
        great gods, an offering."
After him (the priest) to Adar in like manner thus he shall say—
    Oh, Adar, great lord, the strength of fortresses, an offering."

After him (the priest) to Gula in like manner he shall say
" Oh, Gula, mother, begetting mankind, an offering."
After him (the priest) in like manner to Bilat he shall say—
" Oh, Bilat, renowned goddess, wife of Bel, an offering."
After him (the priest) in like manner to Bel he shall say—
" Oh, Bel, most high, establisher of laws, an offering."

Another feature in Babylonian religious services is to be noticed. This is the grand processions of the gods, which took place upon festivals or in time of trouble. We have a reference to these processions in the Chronicle tablet I have already quoted, and also on a fine sculptured slab, formerly in the Museum at Bristol, but now in the British Museum, where we have one of these processions represented in which the gods are being carried in their arks or shrines.

Of the vestments worn by the priest, we have as yet little information. The representation of priests on the seals, notably those on the Egibi tablets, show them with shaven heads, wearing a plain robe resembling the Ephod, bound with a girdle (W. A. I., Vol. V., pl. 56), as did the Jewish priests (Exod. xxviii. 6-12), while the mitre may be contrasted with the curious conical headdress worn by a Babylonian priest in one of the sculptures representing the Babylonian war of Assur-bani-abla (Assyrian Basement, No. 91-94), where a Babylonian priest approaches the king. From an inscription now in the Museum, we learn that the king, in his character of Pontifex Maximus, wore a breast-plate adorned with

twelve precious stones. The position which the
priests occupied in Chaldea was a very high one.
They stood next in precedence to the king, who was
himself head of their order, and in Babylonia they
were a veritable race of Oriental cardinals, and often
very severe thorns in the side of the kings.

The revenue of the priests in Chaldea, as in Egypt
and in India, were derived from tithes payable in
kind, and also from temple estates, resembling the
Wakif Estates, belonging to Arab mosques. In the
inscription of Agu-kak-rimi (W. A. I., Vol. V., pl.
33, col. 7), the king speaks of " A band of youths,
with a portion of a house, field, and garden," dedicated to the temple of Merodach and Zirat-banit."
Also, in the inscription of Nabu-abal-iddina, certain
lands are appointed by the king for the support of
the temple of the Sun god in Sippara. The youths,
who are called *Abli ummani*, literally " sons of the
army"—that is, those who were capable of bearing
arms, formed the temple guard. In a list of guards
(W. A. I., Vol. V., pl. 31), we have mention made of
the *Matzir bit ili*, "the temple guard;" and in an
unpublished fragment, the guard of the great temple
of Assur was stated to be twenty-five men.

It was not only in its religious position that the
temple was so important a feature in the ancient
cities of Chaldea—it was also an important element
in the civil polity. The discovery made by Mr
Rassam at Aboo Hubba of some thousands of tablets,

relating to fiscal, legal, and commercial transactions, show that the temple was the great record office of the State, and that all documents of this character were preserved by the priests. Of the careful way in which such documents committed to their charge were preserved, a remarkable example is again furnished by the result of Mr Rassam's excavations. On the south-east side of the large quadrangle at Aboo Hubba was a smaller square, in which were a series of chambers, evidently offices of the temple. In one of these over thirty thousand tablets were found stored. They were packed as found, and removed to England; and when the cases were opened, it was discovered that the majority of the tablets, except where accidentally displaced, were arranged chronologically. Ranging, as these tablets did, from B.C. 625-200, they must have, for nearly two thousand years, lain buried in the ruins, and quite undisturbed. The temple was also the Court of Justice, and as the Jewish Sanhedrim met in the temple, so did the council (βουλη) of the "grey-haired ones" meet to answer judgment in the courts of the Chaldean temples. Of this custom, we have a curious example in a tablet dating from about B.C. 2120. In this tablet we have a deed of partnership, which was arranged and ratified before the Judges in the temple of the Sun god, in the city of Larsa, in Southern Chaldea, and in which we meet with the following exposition of brotherly love :—

" Brother from brother should not turn away —should not be
    angry over any matter ; a brother to his brother should
    converse ; any thing *in toto* he should not possess."

In concluding this sketch of the Chaldean temple,
we may see how much light it throws on the Hebrew
temple and its services. Similar in construction, with
similar services, sacrifices, and offerings, its prayers
expressing the same ideas often in identical words,
the information thus acquired cannot be neglected
by those who would rightly understand the symbolism and esoteric meaning of the Hebrew ritual.
It is also evident, even by such a slight study as we
have been able to devote to it, how very important
the temple was in the ancient city and state, and
that, if we would seek to restore the life of those
long-silent men, it is to the temple that we must first
direct our steps.

Lecture II.

THE CREATION LEGENDS.

THE position occupied by the cosmogonic legends of an ancient people in their sacred literature is one which is often mistaken. Instead of being the earliest products of the pens of the priest scribes, they are often the latest, or at the least, of a period when the religious belief of the people had attained some considerable degree of development. The examination of the series of legends, which form the subject of this afternoon's lecture, shows them rather to occupy the position of the literature of a period in the growth of religion in Babylonia, when the weird magical Animism of the Akkadians had become influenced by and blended with the purer creed of the Semetic settlers in Chaldea, and out of this fusion was growing up that great and powerful religious system of the Chaldean people. The sacred literature of Chaldea offers many advantages to the student of the origin and development of religious beliefs, not obtainable from the study of other systems. There has been preserved to us in the large series of magical litanies and incantations the books of that creed of Animism, which the Akkadians had brought with them from their mountain home. In that creed we find traces of the child-like efforts of these primitive people to solve the problems of their own existence. Having, by comparison with the human body in sleep and death, arrived at the theory that all being was due to the presence of an indwelling spirit or power, called by them Zi— " life" or " breath," which was temporarily absent in sleep, but never returned in case of death, they proceeded to apply this theory of Animism to the world of nature. The wind, the trees, clouds, the rivers, streams, the sun, moon, and stars, became the abodes of so many indwelling spirits, to whom all their movements and actions were due. This spirit-world soon became divided into two parties of good and evil spirits—those who were beneficial or malevolent to man, and thus the stage of dualism was reached. In course of time, as man proceeded with his study of the phenomena of nature, and their relation to one another, the various elements became grouped—a result which was only attained by long and close observation. The clouds, sun, moon, and stars became the elements, ruled by the great Spirit of Heaven, as the streams, rivers, and metals formed the Kingdom of the Spirit of the underworld. It is evident, from the study of the inscriptions of this Religio-Magical creed, that the purer creed of the Semites from their desert home in Arabia exercised a powerful influence in the work of simplification. The ruling spirits now became gods, and the pantheon was rapidly assuming order and system. A second element, which exercised a powerful influence in the development of the creation legends, was that of the relationship between Light and Darkness. To these ancient thinkers, Darkness was the womb out of which Light came—the mother of all things. Trees, flowers, animated existence of all kinds, were, by the aid of Light, brought forth from the enthralling power of Darkness. It was from this idea of the great primeval night that the idea of that state of chaos which existed before the work of creation had begun was developed.

Of the various series of cosmogonic legends of ancient religious systems, three have always been prominent as the most systematic and highly developed—the Hebrew version as contained in the Book of Genesis, the Chaldean as preserved in the writings of the Greco-Chaldean historians, Berossus and Damascius, and the Phœnician cosmogonic fragments preserved by Sanchoniatho. In each of these three Western Asiatic systems, we find points in common, which, if they do not indicate a common parentage, at least show striking similarity of thought. The fragmentary and late version of the Chaldean creation legends, which had come down to us in the few quotations from the Books of Berossus, bore a very close resemblance to the opening chapters of the Mosaic Books. This resemblance is found to be still more striking, now that we can compare the Hebrew version with the older and original tablets from which Berossus had derived his version. Ten years have now elapsed since Mr George Smith, by the discovery of these important tablets, added additional laurels to the wreath he had already gained by the discovery and decipherment of the Deluge tablet. During that time, Assyriology has made great and important advances. In England, such students, as Professor Sayce and M. M. Pinches and Budge, have brought their knowledge to bear upon this important section of Assyrian literature ; while, on the Continent, Schrader, Delitzsch, Oppert, and Lenormant have also devoted much study to these legends. The result has been that hidden meanings and niceties of expression, not recognised by the "too soon lost" discoverer, have been brought out, and the work of comparison can now be carried out with much more favourable results. Even at the very commencement of our study of these inscriptions, we are met by a small fragment of external evidence, striking in its similarity to the Hebrew version. The system under which the tablets are arranged is by naming the series after the opening words of the first tablet of the series. The first tablet, of which we possess a portion, commences with the words *Enuva Elis*, "In the time when above." And so we find Tablet V. of the series numbered by the Assyrian scribes as "Tablet V. *Enuva Elis*," deriving its name in the same manner as the First Book of Moses is called in the Hebrew Beresheth, or in the Greek Genesis, from its opening words. Of the tablets of this series, we have now portions of four, three of which are, strictly speaking, creation legends—the fourth, of which we have both Babylonian and Assyrian editions, being, as Mr Budge has pointed out, a poem describing the war in heaven.

TABLET I.

1. In the time when above the heavens were unnamed (and),
2. Below for the earth a name was not recorded.
3. The limitless abyss, the first-born, was around them.
4. The chaotic sea was the genetrice of them all.
5. Their waters were joined in one.
6. No crop had been gathered ; no flower had opened.
7. In the time when as yet none of the gods had come forth.
8. By name they were not named ; order [did not exist].
9. The great gods were then made.
10 The gods Lakhmu and Lakhamu caused themselves to come forth, and they spread abroad.
11. The gods Assar and Kisar [were made].
12. They were prolonged many days.
13. The gods Anu (Bel and Hea, were born),
14 The gods Assar and Kissar.

A very casual examination of this fragment is sufficient to reveal its importance, both as affording a striking resemblance to the cosmogonic legends of the Phœnicians and of the Hebrews. It is evident that, like the Hebrew tradition, the Chaldean contained the same idea of the existence of the earth prior to the commencement of the work of creation, in a state of chaos and darkness. This conception is hardly so fully apparent from the rendering of the opening verses of Genesis in our authorised version

B

" In the beginning God created the heaven and
the earth: and the earth was without form and void,
and darkness was upon the face of the deep;" as
the words *tohu va bohu* admit of a more definite rendering than "without form and void," as may be seen
when we compare passages in which the former word
occurs, and also by comparison with Assyrian inscriptions. In Deuteronomy xxxii. 10—" He found
him in a desert land, and in a *waste-howling wilder-
ness;*" and in Job xxvi. 7. we have two examples of
this word—" He stretcheth out the north over the
empty place;" and in Job vi. 18, where our version
again requires emendation, to read—" The caravans
turn aside on their way; they go into the desert and
perish." From the comparison of these passages, it
is evident that we must adopt, as a better rendering in
this passage, " desert " in the place of " without
form." Upon the second word, the Assyrian inscriptions throw some light. One of the most
important goddesses of the Babylonian pantheon was
the goddess called Bahu. She was the spouse of the
water god Hea, and was the goddess who presided
over the south of Babylonia, the region of the
marshes. She bore the title of the " great mother,"
the " noble lady," the " bearing mother of
mankind;" and, in her ancient nature-form, she
was the goddess of the marshy stagnant wastes.
She assumes many of the attributes of the goddess mentioned in this creation tablet—*Mūmu*

Tiamat, the Chaotic Sea, the mother of all nature. We may therefore assume that the rendering of the opening words of Genesis may be taken as— " Then the earth was desert and waste (or marsh)." If we turn to the Assyrian tablet, we see how this idea is substantiated—" The waters were joined in one ; no crop had been gathered, no flower had opened." The word used here for gathered- *Kitstsura*, from *Katsâru*, " to bind or collect "[1]— gives the key to the meaning of the first word, which is unfortunately an *apax legonenis*. The word used for flower is the word usually employed for *lily* or marsh plant, and so the *simile* is preserved. " The crop had not been gathered ;" the earth was like the unproductive desert, and even the marsh land had not borne its typical flower, " the lily "—all was desert and waste. Such was the state of nature, and around all was the *Absu*, or " limitless sea of space." It is somewhat difficult to ascertain the exact nature of this very important element in the Chaldean theogony. In the version of this tablet, given by the Greek Neoplatonic writer, Damascius (Hodges Cory., p. 92), we read—" The Babylonians, like the rest of the barbarians, pass over in silence the *one* principle of the universe, and they constitute two, Taute and Apason, making Apason the husband of Taute, and denominating her ' the mother of the gods.' From these proceeds an only-begotten son, Moymis ;

---

[1] From which the word *Kitsrituv*, " harvest," is derived.

from them also is derived other progeny—Dakhe and
Dakhos, and again a third—Kissare and Assaros ;
from the last of which three others proceed—Anus,
Illinus, and Aus."

In both the cosmogonies of Damascius and of Sanchoniatho, the place of this Absu is the first in the
work of creation. In some cases, Absu, as the
tablets show, is to be identified with the Ætherial
ocean, which circled round the world; but in this
inscription, as well as in some of the hymns, the
priests and theologians of Chaldea have attributed a
more philosophical meaning to it. In the Syllabaries
we find the group Zu-ab explained by *Ab-su*, and an
analysis of this Akkadian compound word affords some
important light. The first element, Zu (No. 25 Sayce
Sylb.), is explained by *idu*, "to know," *lamadu*, "to
teach," and by *mudu*, "knowledge," while the second,
Ab (No. 44 Sayce Sylb.), is explained by *bitu*, "a
house," or *tiamtu*, "the sea," or *abū*, "a cave." So
that the whole compound word may mean "the
house of knowledge" or "the sea of knowledge," and
this we find confirmed by a beautiful Assyrian lit-
any (W.A.I., vol. iv., p. lix., 34-35). We read *Absu
labdhur bit nimiki*, "May Absu, the house of wisdom,
pardon ;" and in the next line we read, *Zukhi labdhur
kabū absu*, "May Zukhi, the depth of the absu,
pardon," which at once may be read, "Oh, may
Zukhi, the depth of the house of wisdom, pardon."
We may then compare with this explanation of

this first-born of creation the following remarkable words in Proverbs viii. 21-27, "The Lord
formed me in the beginning of his way, before
his works of old. I was formed from everlasting,
from the beginning, or ever the earth was. When
there were no depths, I was brought forth ; when
there were no fountains abounding in water. Before
the mountains were settled, before the hills were
brought forth. While as yet he had not made the earth,
or the fields, or the beginning of the dust of the
world. When he prepared the heavens I was there ;
when he set a compass on the face of the deep."
The comparison of these passages with the opening
lines of the tablet almost compel us to adopt the
more philosophical rendering of *absu* here as "wisdom."
Additional support is given to this rendering by comparing the Hebrew and Phœnician legends. The
first-born in the cosmogony of Sanchoniatho by the
union of Apason and Chaos is Desire, and we may
compare with this the expression in Genesis i. 2,
where our authorised version, as I have already said,
misses the beauty. "The breath or spirit of the
Lord brooded on the face of the waters." In the
above extract the deep is rendered by *tehom*, the
exact equivalent of the *tiamat* of the tablet. The
" Spirit of God," the *Rūakh Elohim* of the Hebrew
writers has moreover in many places this philosophic
sense of Divine Wisdom, as in Exodus xxxi. 3, " Behold I have filled him with the Spirit of God, in

wisdom and understanding and in knowledge ; " and the attribute of prophecy is also frequently attributed to the Spirit, as in the case of the inspiration of Balaam (Numb. xxiv. 2), of Saul (1 Saml. x. 6), the messengers of Saul (1 Saml. xix. 20, 23), and the Messiah (Isa. xlii. 1). The comparison of these passages with the Assyrian Absu—the abode of knowledge—enables us to ascertain the reason that led the late Neoplatonic philosophers to make the mind or wisdom an important element in their theogonies. In like manner the Chaotic sea—the Mūmmu Tiamat of the tablet—"the bearing mother of all," the Taute of Damascius, the Tisallat of Berossus, and the bride of Apason underwent many changes as the religion developed. Here she is called the genetrice or "bearing mother" of all; in the Cutha tablet she appears as the "mother" or "nurse" (*muscnik*). In the nature aspect of this character we see the dark watery sea of all-shrouding cloud which surrounded the earth—an aspect of her character, which, in later times, became that of the goddess Bahu, of whom I have already spoken. As the serpent coils round its eggs, so this chaos-serpent lay coiled round the earth, until slain by Merodach, the Lord of Light, who, like Apollo, went forth to slay the Python. The representations which we have of this demon of Chaos show her as a woman with full breasts, like the Asiatic mother-goddess represented in a sculpture at Carchemish—or the Istar

Nana of Babylonians and the Ephesian Diana, as denoting her character of the great Mother and Nurse of all. On a curious boundary-stone, dating from the 12th century before our era, we have a very remarkable figure in which the serpent type is preserved, the body being that of a woman, the lower extremities replaced by the coiled tails of two serpents, like the figures in the sculptures of the Giganto-Machia at Pergamos. It was this Queen of Chaos who ruled while the earth lay like the cosmic egg in her coils, in the "time when as yet none of the gods had come forth."

We now come to the creation of the gods. It is important here to notice that the expression used of these two creations has a reflexive sense —of self-creations "caused themselves to come forth;" they "spread abroad." These two deities, apparently male and female, are named Lakhmu and Lakhamu, and we must certainly identify them with the Dakhe and Dakhos of the cos-mogony of Damascius. At one time I was inclined to identify these creations with deifications of the light, and especially of the first pure light inde-pendent of sun or moon, the first work of the creator (Gen. i. 3). It is more probable now, I think, that that victory of the Divine Light over the power of darkness is represented in the tablet of the War in Heaven, which forms one of the books of this Crea-tion series. I was then inclined to think that the struggle between the two conflicting elements was embodied in the names of these gods, they meaning "the strugglers," from *lakham*, "to fight." It seems to me now that we have rather to take the names as Semitic, meaning "the dividers," and that they correspond to the division of nature into the terrestrial and celestial kingdoms—the Heaven being the firmament dividing the god-land from the Earth. This identification seems to me, though not so fascinating as my former suggestion, to be more in accordance with the spirit of the text. It meets too with strong support from a bilingual list of gods (W. A. I., iii., pl. lxix., 14, 15), in which both these divinities are given as equivalent to the god Anu and his wife Anatu—the Chaldean Zeus and his wife—the deifications of the Heaven. Had they been deifications of the Light we should most probably have found them equated with the Sun god. The two realms of nature are now divided by the firmament; and the next creation is that of the two creatures, Sar or Assar and Kiassar or Kisar—the Assor and Kissare of Damascius. These are two compounds, words composed An-sar or "Heaven host" and Ki-sar, "Earth host," they being the host of Heaven and Earth, the spirit-forms afterwards known as the Annunaki and Ilgi; and upon this we have some light thrown in the expression in Gen. ii. 1.—"Thus the heavens and the earth were finished—all the *host of them*." The Annunaki or

Spirits of Heaven in many ways resemble the " Zabaoth-ha-shamain " of the Bible, which in many places cannot mean the stars. The realm of nature is now so far ready for the three great gods to take possession, and we see the next step in the creation is that of the first trinity of the Babylonian Pantheon—Anu, Ellu or Bel, and Hea, the Anus Illinus and Aus or Oes of Damascius. Of these three great gods little need be said; their epithets mark them as a trinity having both a natural and a philosophical constitution. Anu is called " The Father of all the Gods," " The Progenitor, who changes not the decree coming forth from his mouth," " The Mighty Chief," " The Supreme, the Magnificent," " The Lord of Heaven," " The Heaven." In his character as a Nature-god we find him approaching near to the Vedic Varuna, the Greek Ouranos; while in his religio-philosophic character, according to the Neoplatonicean school, he was the type of " the great father of all "—the Dyaus-pitar or Jupiter of the Pantheon. The second member, Bel or Elu, is a deity of great importance. His most frequent epithets are—" Lord of the world," " The Lord who guards his country," " Establisher of riches and wealth and possessions," " Lord of the lofty place." This last epithet applies to his dwelling on the " Mount of the World—the Mountain of the East "—the Akkadian and Assyrian Olympus. One of his most interesting and important titles was that of *Sadu rabu* or *Saku rabu*, "Most High God," which Dr. Fr. Delitzsch has so well suggested may be the explanation of the *El Shadai*, the "Most High God" of the Hebrews. As a ruler and director of all, he was the *Potentia* of the religio-philosophic triad. The last member of this triad is one of the most important gods in the whole pantheon. He is called the "Lord of the Earth;" he was the "Lord of the Sea," the "Lord of the Absu (House of Wisdom)," the "Lord of the Bright Eye (Far-seeing)," the "Lord of the noble Incantation;" but he was chiefly celebrated for his wisdom. In the inscriptions we find him consulted by all the gods in times of trouble, as in the tablet of the War against the Moon (W. A. I. iv., 5, 37, 54) we read that when the god Bel saw the trouble afflicting the Moon, he called to his messenger, Nusku, the god of "the morning star."—"Bel to his messenger, Nusku, spoke: 'My messenger, this message to the Absi (House of Wisdom) take—The message that the Moon God in Heaven fearfully is troubled, to Hea in the Absi tell. Nusku the command of his Lord obeyed. To Hea, in the Absi, as a swift messenger, he hastened. To Hea the Master, the Supreme Ruler, the Unchangeable Lord, Nusku, he command of his Lord told.'" The Deluge tablet brings out more emphatically his character for wisdom. After the cataclysm we read Bel was angry that some had escaped the Deluge by means of the ark, and asks of his companion-god, Adar, who taught

men to build the ark? upon which the reply is—
"Who, except Hea, can form a design? Yea, Hea
knows all things, and he teaches (them)." We see,
therefore, that as "the god of metals, the god of the
rivers and streams," he is Pluto and Cronos of the
mythological triad, and the Mens of the philosophical.
From this small fragment we get the following table
of the Birth of the Gods:—

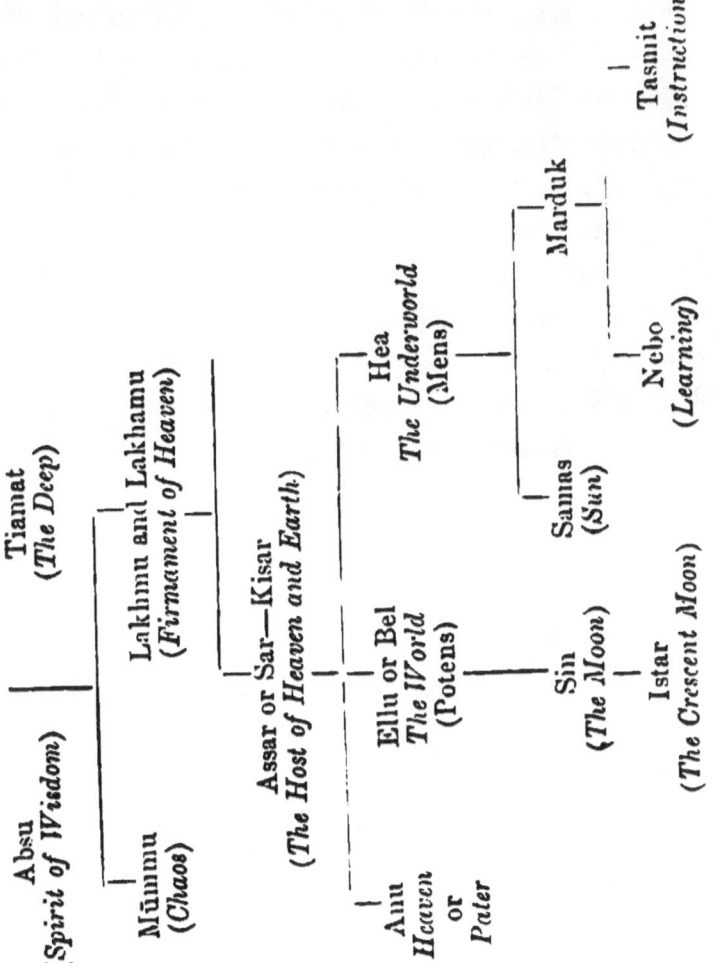

The examination of this fragment shows that it presents a close and remarkable agreement in many points with both the Phœnician and Hebrew theogonic legends. With regard to the latter we may say that its parallelisms are to be found in the creations of the first two days (Gen. i. 1-9).

We now pass to the other tablets of the series. There is no tablet corresponding to the work of the third day (Gen. i. 9-13); but the fifth tablet of the series, which corresponds to the work of the fourth day in the Hebrew account (Gen. i. 14-23), is very fortunately the best preserved of the series. The careful way in which this tablet was drawn up, and its detailed analysis of the arrangement of the heavenly bodies, throws very great light upon the date and character of these tablets. The text of the tablet, which is published, Delitzsch-Assyriologische Lesestucke, pl. 76. is well preserved in the obverse, though the reverse is unfortunately lost.

FIFTH TABLET.

1. He made pleasant the dwelling places of the great gods.
2. The constellations their forms as animals he fixed.
3. The year its divisions he divided.
4. Twelve months of constellations by threes He fixed,
5. From the day when the year began to its end.
6. He determined the place of the crossing stars, and the seasons their bounds;
7. Not to make fault or error of any kind.
8. The positions of Bel and Hea, he established with his own.

9. He opened great gates in the side of the world :
10. The bolts he made strong on the left hand and the right.
11. In the mass he made an ascent.
12. The Illuminator (Moon-god) he made to shine, to rule the night.
13. He appointed it also to establish the night until the coming forth of day.
14. Every month, without fail, by its disk he regulated.
15. In the beginning of the month, at the rising of the night
16. Horns shine forth to lighten the heavens.
17. On the Seventh day a circle it approaches.
18. To divide the dawns, he appointed (it—?)
19. When the Sun on the horizon of heaven at Thy coming.

At the first inspection of this tablet it is evident that we have before us a document of the highest importance, full of remarkable agreement with the Hebrew tradition, and at the same time presenting us with several striking divergences. With the confused account of the Phœnician priest it presents very little agreement, and the fragment of Berossus in correspondence with it being lost, our comparative studies are confined to the Hebrew record. The opening words of the fourth day in the Mosaic account (Gen. i., 14, 15) present a contrast which perhaps does not appear at first—"And God said, Let there be lights in the firmament of the heaven, to divide the day from the night, and let them be for signs and for seasons and for days and years." And then a little further on we read, "He made two great lights, the greater light to rule the day and the lesser light to rule the night: He made the stars

also." Here we have a distinct reversal of the
Assyrian order of creation.   In the tablet we find
the stars created first, and arranged in groups for the
measurement of time, and the Moon, the greater
light, for the measurement of the month and the
night, and the Sun, the lesser light, for the measurement of the day and the year—a sequence which is
an exact reversal of the Hebrew one.   It is in these
varying arrangements that we get very important
matter to enable us to contrast the two accounts, and
in some measure to approximate their relative ages.
It is clear that the Babylonian or Assyrian tablet
exhibits a more than rudimentary knowledge of the
science of astronomy, as we have before us in these
15 lines—(1) The arrangement of the constellations
according to the signs of the zodiac; (2) The marking of the four crossing points on the great circle,
the solstices and equinoxes; (3) The Lunar phases.
Another important point to be noticed is the prominence given to the moon over the sun, and the particular details as to the calculation of the length of
the night.   The preference which is given to the
moon over the sun here brings us in contact at once
with one of the most interesting sections of the
growth of religion, and the changes that a religion
passes through as a nation advances from one stage of
national life to another.   In his very valuable paper
on the Astronomy and Astrology of the Babylonians
(Trans. Soc. Bib. Arch., vol. iii., p. 207), Professor

Sayce thus speaks of the priority of the moon over the sun: "As befitted a nation of astronomers, the moon was considered prior to the sun, and the originator of civilisation." It is hardly in this way that we can explain the priority. Turning to the astronomical tablets, we gain a little insight into the reason: we find that the name given to the planets by the Akkadians of Lu-Bat was translated by the Assyrians by *Tseni*, "sheep," the Hebrew *tsôn* (Tran. Soc. Bib. Arch., vol. v., pp. 44 and 375), and also by *bibū*, literally "bright eyes," and also *ailu* or *ailim*, "bell-wethers," or leaders of the flock. In like manner we find a star, which I am inclined to regard as the pole-star, called "The Star of the flock of many sheep of the Spirit of Heaven;" and we meet with the expression, "stars like sheep," in the tablet of the War in Heaven. Turning now to the Hebrew Scriptures, we find this pastoral nomenclature employed as indicated by the phrase, "He telleth the number of the stars and giveth them all their names" (Psl. cxlvii. 4), but it never assumes the prominence it does among other nations, especially the Arabs. The description of Arab thought in relation to the bright, starry, and moonlit heaven is so graphic, and so explanatory of the inscriptions, that it must be quoted:—"With the refreshing dews of evening, not Venus only or the moon, but the whole glory of the starry heavens met the eye and touched the spirit of the Arabs. High above the tents and resting flocks, above the nocturnal raid and waiting ambuscade, and all the doings of men, the stars passed along on their glittering courses. They guided the Arabs on their way through the desert; certain constellations announced the wished-for rain; others the wild storm, the changes of season, the time for breeding in the flocks. Hence to tribes of the desert especially brilliant stars appeared as living spirits, as rulers over nature and the fortunes of mankind." An Arab poet (Al Nabigâ, iii., 2) uses the beautiful expression, "A night so long . . . that I say to myself, 'It has no end, and the Shepherd of the Stars will not come back to day.'" In the Babylonian astronomical tablets we meet with a similar pastoral tone; indeed throughout the tablets there are hardly any omens relating to cities. To quote a few examples— "The star on high rises to clouds, and rain it points;" "The star of the eagle is observed, the cattle decrease." Such an omen as the following (W.A.I., vol. iii., pl. 64)—"The moon at its appearance with the rising sun is seen: The gods the fields of the land to evil assign: Bel courage to the enemy gives"—points directly to a tribal raid at a time when the moon rises late in the morning, leaving long dark evenings, under cover of which the Bedouin could advance. In these omens we find similar thoughts to those of the Arabs, and ample evidence that it is to a nomadic people we owe such an arrangement as there is in this tablet. It was not, says Speigel, the sun that first attracted the savage by its sight; it was the night sky with its lights, in contrast to the dark earth. So the moon is a friend to the nomad and shepherd : it gives him bright nights to travel or dark nights for his raids, whereas the sun dries up his water and pasturage. The direct ascendency of the moon is again indicated in a bilingual hymn (Del. Lesestucke, pl. 16), where the goddess Istar, as the morning star, is thus addressed by the worshipper—"Of thy father, the moon god, and thy brother, the sun," making the moon father of the sun. The opening lines of this tablet relate to the arrangement of the stars for the measurement of the year :—

1. The constellations their forms as animals he fixed.
2. The year its divisions he divided,
3. From the day when the year commences to its end.
4. Twelve months of constellations by threes he fixed.
5. He determined the place of the crossing stars, to the seasons their bounds ;
6. Not to make fault or error of any kind.
7 The abode of Bel and Hea he appointed with his own.

The division of the great circle into twelve divisions, through which the sun passed in his yearly journey, is proved by additional matter in the inscriptions. In a large astronomical tablet relating to the divisions of the year, we read (W.A.I., Vol. iii., pl. 53)—"Twelve months to each year, 360 (60 × 6) days in number, are recorded." Again, a few lines on, we read—"The rising and appearance of the moon for the month one watches; the balancing of the stars and the moon and (their) opposition one watches. For the year its months, for the months their days—the tale is made complete." Also, "The twelve months in full, from the beginning to the end, to the measure of days fixed." In the Deluge tablet, (col. iii. 30, 31)—"I looked to the regions bounding the sea, to the twelve points no land." It requires but a very casual examination of the arrangement of the Akkadian calendar, and the accompanying series of the Twelve Legends of Gizdhubar, to see that the calendar is arranged according to a zodiac of twelve constellations similar to our own. For example, the second month is called the month of the Propitious Bull, corresponding to the sign of Taurus; the third the month of the Twins, corresponding to Gemini; the eleventh the month of the Curse of Rain, corresponding to the sign of Aquarius. According to this same tablet (Rev. 8), "the beginning of the year appears to have been fixed by the rising of the star Icu or Dilgan, which was the patron star of Babylon (W.A.I. ii. 47), though it is difficult to identify it with any special star. As we learn from this fifth Creation Tablet, the great circle was divided into four parts of three months each, and the division points were marked by the Nibiru or crossing stars that marked the equinox and solstice points. There

THE CREATION LEGENDS.

51

are two reasons which lead me to adopt this rendering. In a tablet giving the names of the star of Merodach, during the twelve months we find that in the month Tasrituv, that is September, he is called *Nibiru*, and this month marks the period when the sun, at the autumnal equinox, passes from the one half of the year to the other. The second argument is furnished by an unpublished tablet (S. 1907), which gives the seasons of the Babylonian year, and this fragment also explains the division into positions of the three great gods mentioned in line 8 of the tablet.

1st Season lost, but we can see from the fragment that it extended from the 1st day of Adar (Feb.-Mar.) to the 20th day of Airu (Ap.-May), and was the season of rain and sunshine. The latter rain of the Jewish calendar.

2nd Season—"From the 1st day of Sivan (May–June) to the 30th day of Ab (July-Aug.), the sun is in the course of Bel, the season of crops and fruits." This was the wheat harvest and fruit season in Palestine. The feast of first-fruits falling in Sivan.

3rd Season—"From the 1st day of Elul (Aug.-Sept.) to the 30th day of Marchesvan (Oct.-Nov.), the sun is in the course of Anu, the season of rain and clouds." This was the period of the former or autumnal rains in Palestine.

4th Season—"From the 1st day of Kislev (Nov.-Dec.) to the 30th day of Sabadhu (Jan.-Feb.), the sun is in the course of Hea, the season of storms." This was the winter season of Palestine.

We may conclude from these passages that either the Nibiru were the equinoxes and solstices, or the constellations marking commencement of each of these four seasons.

The analysis of the opening lines of the fifth tablet shew very clearly that in the Chaldean, as in the Hebrew cosmogony, the stars and lights were created to be for signs and for seasons, and for days and years.

I now pass to the creation of the moon, the greater light according to the Babylonian teaching.

1. He opened great gates in the side of the world.
2. The bolts he made strong on the left hand and on the right.
3. In the mass he made an ascent.
4. The Illuminator (the Moon-god) he caused to shine, to rule throughout the night.
5. He appointed it also, to establish the night until the coming forth of day.
6. Every month, without fail, by its disk he appointed.
7. In the beginning of the month, at the rising of the night,
8. Horns shine forth to lighten the heavens.
9. On the 7th day to a circle it approaches.
10. To divide the dawns he established (it).
11. At that time the sun on the horizon of heaven at thy coming.

The conception in these lines that the heavenly bodies made their entrance and exit from the regions below the horizon through great gates is one common to most ancient eastern mythologies. In the Egyptian Ritual of the Dead we have the fifteen great pylons of the land of Karneter guarded by genii, armed with swords, through which the deceased had to pass, and through which Osiris passed daily. The description of these gates is found in ch. cxlvi. of the Ritual, which bears the title of "The beginning of the Gates of Aahlu, or Fields of Peace." A similar idea is found to be held regarding the rising of the sun by the writer of the Book of Enoch. A fuller exposition of the Chaldean idea is contained in a hymn to the rising Sun-god (W.A.I. iv., pl. 20, No. 2):—

1. Oh Sun-god, on the horizon of heaven thou dawnest.
2. The bolts of the bright heavens thou openest.
3. The folding doors of the heavens thou openest.
4. Oh Sun-god, to the countries thy head thou liftest up.
5. Oh Sun-god, the glory of the heavens over (all) lands thou spreadest.

According to the Gizdhubar Legends, these great gates by which the sun rose and set were guarded by scorpion men, whose "heads reached to the threshold of heaven, and whose footing was in the underworld." "The Illuminator" is the usual title applied to the Moon-god, and in a long hymn to the moon (W.A.I., vol. iv., pl. 9) we find the deity addressed as *Abu Nannar belur ilu dhabu ebili ilani*—"Father Illuminator, Lord and Good God ruling the gods." This name of Nannar no doubt was the origin of the myth of Nannaros related by Ctesias. In the fourth and fifth lines of this section of the tablet—"The Illuminator he caused to shine, to rule throughout the night. He appointed it also, to establish the night until the coming forth of day"—is exactly in accordance with

the Hebrew idea: "And God made two great lights
—the lesser light to rule the night" (Gen. i. 16).
The description of the phases of the moon is now
given; and, as we see, it was held important in
Chaldea, as in Palestine and among the Arabs, to
watch for the new moon, which marked the beginning of the month. Those who have travelled among
these clear-eyed sons of the desert know how much
sooner they espy the small thin crescent than we
with our dull eyes. A number of reports relating to
this watching for the new moon are to be seen among
the astronomical tablets in the British Museum
(W.A.I., vol. iii. pl. li., Nos. 3, 4, 5; pl. liii., No. 3).
For example (li. 3):—"A watch we observe; on
the 29th day the moon we see. May Nebo and
Merodach to the King my Lord draw near. Report
of Nabu of Assur." Another longer report is of
interest, as showing the difficulties under which
the observations were often conducted (pl. li. No.
6):—

> To the King my Lord: Thy servant, Istar-iddina-abla,
> One of the chiefs of the Astronomers of Arbela.
> May there be peace to the King my Lord.
> May Nebo, Merodach, and Istar of Arbela
> To the King my Lord approach.
> On the 29th day a watch we kept.
> The House of Observation was covered with cloud.
> The Moon we did not see.
> Dated month Sebadh (Jany.-Feb.), 1st day in the Eponym
>   year of Bel-Kharran-sadua.

The date of this tablet is fixed by the Eponym Canon as B.C. 649, contemporary with the reign of Manasseh, King of Judah. These tablets show the importance that the Assyrians attached to the observation of the new moon. We may compare this strict watch with the Hebrew customs: "In the day of your gladness, and in your appointed seasons, and in the beginnings of your months, ye shall blow with the trumpets over your burnt-offerings" (Numb. x. 10). "Blow the trumpet in the new moon" (Ps. lxxxi. 3). "New moon and sabbath" (Isa. i. 13). A fuller explanation of the lunar phases is to be found in an astronomical tablet (W.A.I. iii., 55, 3):—

The Moon on its appearance, from the 1st day to the 5th day,
For five days is visible. The Moon is Anu.
From the 6th day to the 10th day, for five days it is full. It is Hea.
From the 11th day to the 15th day, for five days to a crown it grows.
The Moon is Anu, Bel and Hea in its mass.

This tablet, we see, also gives the same division of the lunar orbit as that recorded in line 8, and enables us to identify Anu as the creator of the heavenly bodies. In a hymn to the moon, also, we get the following paragraph in praise of the bright "horns": "Oh, glowing light! whose horns are powerful, whose limbs (rays) are perfect, pure as crystal;" and the beauty of its far spreading light is recorded in these words : " Lord, in thy divine form the remote heavens and wide spreading sea thou fillest with thy reverence." It is extremely unfortunate that the remaining lines relating to the creation of the sun are in so mutilated a condition as to render any connected translation impossible. The path of the sun is mentioned here by the name of *Kharran Samsi;* and the bright god is addressed by the epithet, most frequently applied to him, of the Judge. In the Michaux stones in the Louvre, and in most of the boundary-stone inscriptions, we find this deity, like the Greek Helios, addressed as *Dian Nisi*—"Judge of men." In one example (W.A.I., vol. iii., pl. 42, 19): "Oh, Sun-god, judge of heaven and earth, his face may he smite, and his bright day to darkness may he turn." In other inscriptions we find this idea of the sun as the all-seeing judge more strongly expressed, as in the Cylinder of Tiglath-Pileser i. (B.C. 1120) (W.A.I., vol. i., i.-ix. 7), the sun is called " the patrol surpriser of his enemies, the scatterer of the sheep (stars);" and in an unpublished hymn to Gizdhubar, the solar hero, we find the phrases—" Oh Gizdhubar, perfect king, judge of the spirits, exalted prince, lord of mankind, patrol of the four quarters, recorder of the earth, lord of the underworld. Thou art a judge, and decidest like a god; thou standest upon earth holding judgment—thy judgment is not reversed or thy sentence ignored; thou rulest, thou examinest, thou judgest, thou decidest and governest.

The Sun-god has put the sceptre of decision into thy hand."

This character of the Judge of all is the most important phase of the solar worship of Babylonia, It is referred to in the few mutilated lines of this creation tablet in the words *dina dinu*—"Judgment he judges." The lines already quoted (13)—"He appointed it (the moon) to establish the night, until the coming forth of day,"—show that in this cosmogony, as in that of the Hebrews, the sun was " to rule the day" (Gen. i. 16).

The next tablet is a small fragment forming part of the *Daily Telegraph* collection, which, though very mutilated, evidently corresponds to the work of the sixth day in the Hebrew account (Gen. i. 24, 25), the creation of the cattle and creeping things :—

(1.) When the gods in their assembly had made,

(2.) They made all things pleasant.

(3.) They caused to come forth living creatures.

(4.) The cattle of the field, the beasts of the field, and the creeping things.

(5.) .   .   .   .   .   to living creatures

(6.) The cattle and creeping things of the city they sent forth.

(7.) The assembly of creeping things and all creation,

(8.) .   .   .   which in the assembly of my family.

(9.) .   .   .   .   .   the God of the Holy Eye (Hea), pairs associated.

(10.) .   .   .   The assembly of creeping things he scattered abroad.

Fragmentary and mutilated as this tablet is, it

contains much of importance, and, like the fifth
tablet, affords some indication of the character of the
people who composed the cosmogony. The expression "living creatures," *siknat napiste*, is a near
equivalent of the Hebrew néphesh-khay-yah in Gen.
i. 24, and is used through the Assyrian sacred literature for the expression of animated nature. Like the
fifth tablet, this one was drawn up with great care.
We see the domestic cattle (bulu) distinguished from
the wild animals (umami) of the field, and the latter
are omitted when the animals of the city are spoken
of. The fuller sense of this idea of the wild beast as
distinct from domestic cattle is shown in the obelisk
inscription of Tiglath-Pileser, i. (B.C. 1120) (W.A.I.
i., pl. 28), where we read, "the rest of the numerous
animals (umami), the winged birds of the air, which,
among the beasts of the field, the work of his hands."
In this same text the expression is *umami sa tchamte*,
"beasts of the sea," is used to express some of the
marine monsters captured by the king during his
expedition to the shores of the Mediterranean; so
that this text, although not one of the creation
series, serves to connect the fifth tablet and our
fragment, and to indicate the existence of a similar
account of the fifth day's creation as that found in
the Hebrew version (Gen. i. 20-23). The distinction
in the tablet between the cattle of the field or desert
and those of the city, the priority being given to the
former, bears out what I have already spoken of

regarding the origin of the legends being sought among the nomadic Semites rather than the city-dwelling Akkadians. It is most probable that had we the remainder of this tablet we should have found in it the Assyrian story of the creation of mankind. The deity mentioned here under the title *Nin-Eni-Illute,* "Lord of the bright eye," is the god Hea, and it is to this "all-wise" god that the creation of mankind is attributed. In the tablet which Mr Smith regarded as the Chaldean account of the fall, but which Dr. Oppert has conclusively shown is a hymn to the god Hea, we find the words, "*Ana Padi sunu ibnu arilute,*" "to be obedient to them (the gods) he made mankind;" also, we read, *likuna aima amatu su ina pi zalmat kakkadi sa ibna kata su,* "May his command be established in the mouth of mankind, who his hands have made." In the hymns we often find that Merodach, the son of Hea, who occupies a position but a slight degree inferior to that of his father, often assumes the divine titles and prerogatives of his father, as in the following passage from a hymn :—"The incantation of life is thine, the Philtre of life is thine, the Holy writing of the House of Wisdom (Absu) is thine;" and then the following important passage :—*Avilutuv zalmat kakkadi, siknat napisti mala suma naba ina mate basa,*—"Mankind, (even) the human race, the living creatures, all that by name is called (and) in the land exists is (thine). The four quarters (are thine). The angel host of heaven and earth, all that exist (are thine)" (W.A.I., vol. iv., pl. xxix., No. 1, 30-44). It would appear, therefore, to Hea, or to his son Merodach, or to the pair conjointly, that we must attribute the creation of the human race, and if this is the case, it tends to support very strongly the proposition of Sir Henry Rawlinson that Hea was the god of the section of the Akkadians who in their religious development attained nearest to Monotheism. I need hardly, now that we have reached the end of our examination of these tablets, show how striking in thought and expression, often in identical language, is the resemblance between the Assyrian and the Hebrew accounts. Even that oft repeated refrain of divine satisfaction‘ and " God saw that it was good," finds its counter-part in the phrase occurring in both tablets five and seven,—" *Ubassim*," " He made pleasant." There now remains the very important, but equally difficult, question of the date and relationship of these tablets to the Hebrew account. And here I must ask my readers to bear in mind the fact that I am treating this subject from a purely Assyriological side, leaving the Hebrew side to those more competent to deal with it than myself.

The first point to be noticed is the marked differ-ence between the Creation Tablets and the generality of Assyrian tablets. The majority of the religious tablets, litanies, hymns, prayers, etc., found in the Assyrian royal library at Nineveh, are admittedly

copies from older documents in the temple libraries
of Chaldea, and each bears a colophon or docket on
the reverse, stating it to be *Kima labri su,* "like its
old copy." We find the docket upon all the tablets
of the Gizdhubar Legends, including the Deluge
Tablet; upon the Dibbara Legends, and upon the
bilingual Akkadian and Assyrian hymns, etc. There
are, however, a certain class of tablets which do not
bear this statement, such as the very beautiful series
of Assyrian prayers (W. A. I., vol. iv., pl. 58, 59, 63,
64), and examination of these tablets shows them to
be distinctly Semitic in character, thought, similies,
and language. They may be here and there influenced by Akkadianisms, but they are essentially
different from the magical hymns and formulæ. In
like manner we find the Creation Tablets omit this
colophon. This would seem at first to mark them of
a date as late as B.C. 650, the time when the library
at Nineveh was founded by Assurbanipal. This cannot be admitted in the face of further evidence from
beneath the dust of ages. Among the fragments of
tablets obtained by Mr Rassam and others from the
excavations in the Birs Nimroud, the site of the
ancient temple of Nebo, the god of learning, are
some duplicate copies of the Creation Tablets, portions of the fifth, and also a large tablet of the series
relating to the War in Heaven. At the same time
duplicates of other texts, grammatical tablets, and
the Deluge Tablet, in the library of Nineveh, have

been obtained from the excavations at Birs Nimroud and Aboo Hubba. The character of the writing and the arrangement of the texts, as well as the historical impossibility—the library at Nineveh probably being in ruins at the time when the tablets were written, in the reigns of Nebuchadnezzar and Nabonidus (B.C. 604-555)—would militate seriously against the Babylonian version being copied from the Assyrian. We must therefore conclude that copies were in the Babylonian libraries prior to B.C. 660, and it was from these that the later copies, as well possibly as the Assyrian versions, were made. The advanced knowledge of astronomy exhibited in the fifth tablet brings us in close contact with the astronomical tablets. It is evident from the definite and accurate description of the comet of about the year 1120 B.C. given in the tablets (W. A. I., iii., 52, 1) that as early as the 12th century Baylonian astronomy was in a very high state of development. The writers of the tablets attribute the compilation of the important series of astronomical tablets entitled "The Book of the Illumination of Bel," to Sargon of Akkad, whose date is now fixed as B.C. 3750. This may be only a mythical story; but if the tablet of the Wars of Sargon and Naram-Sin (W. A. I., vol. iv., pl. 34) is, as it appears to be, a genuine copy of a Babylonian document, there is more proof of its truth than at first appears. By the

arrangement of the Gizdhubar legends according to
the signs of the Zodiac, and the Equinoxial Festivals
in the Sacrificial Tablet from Aboo Hubba, it appears that the seasons, the equinoxes, etc., had been
observed and used as time measurers as early as B.C.
2400.   I have already pointed out that the prominence given to the moon and stars in the fifth,
and the distinction made in the seventh between the
animals of the plain and town, marks the influence
of the nomadic life upon the thoughts of the com-
pilers of these tablets.   We may now turn to a very
remarkable series of tablets dating in the reign of
Khammurabi, whose date Mr Pinches has established
as B.C. 2120.   In these tablets we get a series of
proper names of a remarkable character, such as
Abil, Kainuv, Ismi-ilu, which resemble the Hebrew
Abel, Cain, and Ishmael; but also we have such
names as *Ilu bani*, "God has made," *Ana-pani-ilu*,
"To the face of God," *Ilu iddina*, "God has given,"
while many hundreds of names occur in which the
name of the Moon-god is the most prominent element.   The evidence to be deduced from these tablets is, that as early as the twenty-second century
before the Christian era there were living in the
neighbourhood of Ur and Larsa the Ellassar of Gen.
xiv., 1.—a population speaking a language akin to
that of the Hebrews, worshipping an abstract deity,
the *Ilu El* of the Hebrews, the *Allah* of the Arabs,

and in their pantheon placing the Moon-god in the foremost place. May not these ancestors, and possibly companions, of Abraham, have known at least the elements of these traditions of the Beginnings of all things ?

Lecture III.

"ASSYRIAN PALACES."

IF in the older motherland of Chaldea it is to the temple we turn for the memorials of some ancient city, in Assyria, the northern kingdom of Mesopotamia, it is in the palaces of the great king that we must look for the records which are to restore to us the memorials of the long buried past. It may be, as M. Perrot has suggested, that the lords of the younger empire, in throwing off the yoke of the southern motherland, had released themselves from the power and traditions of that religious caste which held so strong rule in Chaldea. Be this as it may, the explorations in the mounds of debris which form the graves of the cities of Assur, have shown that beneath these vast tumuli there lie buried the palaces of the kings of Assyria; and where temples have been found, they are subordinate to the larger royal residence. Both scriptural and monumental evidence are at one in proving Assyria to have been a colony and dependency upon the land of Chaldea, which in about the nineteenth

C

century before the Christian era became sufficiently
strong to throw off the yoke of the home country, and
rule as independent. This independence was not
acquired immediately. For a time the rulers still
bore the title of *patesi* or "viceroy," but in the course
of time they assumed the title of king. An additional
proof of the Chaldean origin of the cities of Assyria,
which, like Chaldea, began its history with a tetrapolis
of Assur, Nineveh, Calah, and Resen, is that, with the
exception of the last of these, the names do not admit
of explanation by Semetic etymology. The account
given in the book of Genesis (ch. x. 11), in its revised
reading, should be, "Out of that land he (Nimrod)
went forth into Assyria, and builded Nineveh, the
same is the city of streets, and Calah, and Resen
between Calah and Nineveh, the same is a great city."
The accuracy of the passage when contrasted with the
evidence of the monuments is very remarkable, for it
is evident that the writer of these words must have
had some knowledge of the distinctive features of two
at least of the cities. In speaking of the great city
of Nineveh as the city of streets or broadways, he
alludes to the most important feature of the topography
of the Assyrian capital. The Assyrian kings Esarhaddon and his son Assurbanipal both make mention
of the "broadways" or streets of Nineveh in which
they made their captives walk in procession. In the
account of his Zidonian war Esarhaddon says (W.A.I.,
vol. i., col. i. 49-53): "The heads of Sanduarri and

Abdi-milkuti upon the necks of their great men I hung, and together with musicians, male and female, through the streets (*ribit*) of Nineveh I made to pass." In like manner the prophet Nahum—(ch. ii. 4), " The chariots shall rage in the streets, they shall justle one another in the broadways "—seems to have known of this important feature in Ninevite topography. Also, in speaking of the city of Calah, the writer uses the expression, "the same is a great city," a phrase which is an almost exact translation of the ancient name of the city; the Hebrew Calah being only another form of the Assyrian Kalkhu—the Akkadian Kal-khi, "strong city." The city of Resen is mentioned in the Bavian inscription of Sennacherib as a town adjacent to Nineveh. The writer of this passage, describing the rise of Assyria, makes no mention of the city of Assur, the metropolis of the northern kingdom; but in the name given to the district colonised he implies its existence. This name of the most ancient city of the empire, the ruins of which are marked by the lofty mound of Kileh Shergat on the west bank of the Tigris, near the mouth of the lower Zab, is again of non-Semetic origin. On the older bricks the name occurs as Ausar—that is, "the city on the water's bank "—and from a bilingual tablet in the Museum we know that the name Ninua was a Semitic form of the Akkadian *Ni-Na-Ki*, "his resting place." The relative positions of these three cities, Assur, Calah, and Nineveh, situated as they were at important places on the banks of the Tigris, lead us to attribute their origin, in the first place, to stations on one of the military and commercial roads leading northward. This premiss seems to meet with support from an ancient Akkadian name of the city of Assur, which was *Pal-bi-ki*, "the place of his crossing," as it was in the neighbourhood of this city that one of the roads from Babylonia crossed over to the east bank of the Tigris. Assur being the most ancient city of Assyria, its earliest kings bearing the titles of *Patesi Ausar*, as in an inscription of Samsi-Rimmanu on one of the bricks from Kileh Shergat, which reads, "*Samsi-Rammanu patesi Ausar abil Igur-Kapkapu bani Bit Ausar*—"Samsi-Rammanu, son of Igur-Kapkapu, builder of the temple of Ausar" (W.A.I., vol. i., pl. vi. 1); it was very natural that the proud Assyrians should seek to find a divine origin for its foundation. Fragments of this interesting legend are found in a tablet marked K. 3445, which most Assyriologists have hitherto included in the creation series. After describing the god Assur as desirous of creating an abode on earth, the tablet states that that dwelling-place was "the land which thy hands have made, the city *Pal-bi-ki* thou hast called its name." The history of the Assyrian empire, like that of the sister kingdom of Egypt, divides itself into three well-defined periods: (1) The early empire, from about B.C. 1900-1050; (2) the middle empire, from B.C. 891-

722; and (3) the late empire, the period of the
Sargonide dynasty, from B.C. 721-625. Each of these
periods is also identified with a special capital, and it
is besides incidentally important that as the empire
increased in power the capital was removed further
and further north along the Tigris. The early empire
had for its capital the city of Assur, the middle that
of Calah, and the later that of Nineveh; and it is in
the palaces of these cities that we must look for the
records of these ancient cities. Of the capital of the
early empire we know comparatively little — the
isolated nature of the ruins of Kileh Shergat which
mark its site, combined with the extreme solidity of
the vast mass of debris forming its acropolis, have
rendered excavations on the site extremely difficult.
That there was a palace here we know, for Tiglath-
Pileser I. (B.C. 1120) records the repairs he executed
on its walls; but little can be gleaned as to its construction. When, however, we come to study the
royal residences of the middle and later empire, ample
material is accessible to us. In the mound of Nimroud,
situated at the junction of the Tigris with the upper
Zab, and on the east bank of the river, remains of no
less than four or five palaces have been found. The
most ancient appears to have been one built in the
14th century, B.C., by a king named Shalmanesar 1.
Of this we have no architectural details; only a few
bricks remain to prove its existence. The next most
important edifice was the palace situated at the north-

west end of the mound, near to the lofty stage tower
which crowned the south end of the acropolis, which
was built by **Assur-nazir-abla** (B.C. 885-860). Most
of the sculptures from this palace and from the temple
adjoining are now exhibited in the Nimroud gallery
of the British Museum. The south-west palace was
the work of Shalmanesar III., the contemporary of
Ahab and Jehu. Between these two edifices, in about
B.C. 740, Tiglath-Pileser II. built himself a royal
residence, which is known as the central palace.
Sargon, prior to the building of his own splendid
palace at Dur Sargina, the ruins of which are marked
by the mound of Khorsabad, restored portions of the
north-west palace at Calah; and Esarhaddon, late in
his reign, commenced building a palace, using chiefly
materials which he had taken from the other and
older buildings on the mound. The mound of
Koyunjik, opposite the town of Mosul, which marks
the acropolis of Nineveh, has furnished remains of
the palaces of the later empire. This mound is about
a mile and a-half in circumference, and rises to a
height of about 40 feet above the level of the *enceinte*
of the city. The explorations on this site by Sir
Henry Layard, Mr Hormuzd Rassam, and Mr George
Smith, have afforded evidence of the existence of at
least four palaces. The first was an edifice dating as
early as the 14th century, which was repaired by
Shalmanesar I., and by Assur-ris-issi (B.C. 1150) and
his son Tiglath-Pileser I. (B.C. 1120). This ancient

palace was probably occupied by the kings of the middle empire until the erection of the palaces at Calah. Sennacherib (B.C. 705) was the first, however, to erect a royal residence on the mound worthy of Assyria's kings, and the palace situated at the south-east end of the mound, which he built early in his reign, is an edifice exhibiting, both in architecture and ornamentation, a considerable advance on the style of the buildings of the kings of the middle empire. Later in his reign this same king built a palace to the south of the large acropolis, on the spot now marked by the mound of Nebby Yunus. The palace, though every effort has been made by Mr Rassam to commence the work, still awaits exploration. The south-east palace was occupied for a few years by Assur-bani-pal (B.C. 668), who, after his brilliant victories in Egypt and other lands, built for himself a royal abode at the north-west end of the mound; and it is from this palace that the finest remains of Assyrian art have come, and which now adorn the galleries of the British Museum. The sculptures from the palace of Sennacherib are now exhibited in the Koyunjik gallery of the Museum, and those from the palace of Assurbanipal in the basement room. One other palace remains, and this, fortunately, the largest and most thoroughly explored, and it will furnish us with the most ample material for our study of the construction and ornamentation of the palaces of the kings of Assyria.

In the year B.C. 722 Sargon, the tartan, or com-
mander-in-chief, revolted against his master, Shalmanesar IV., and made himself king. At that time,
as I have already stated, the capital and royal residence was in Calah. Fearing, no doubt, the revolt
of the Assyrians, who, like all oriental nations,
required but little cause to rise in rebellion and
sweep a despot from his throne, the usurper determined to build for himself a new palace or palace-
city, which, by its isolated position and strong
fortifications, should afford him shelter from any
sudden outburst of popular feeling. He selected a
spot about nine miles north-east of Nineveh, and
there built a palace-city, an oriental Versailles,
which he called Dur-Sargina—"Fort Sargon,"—the
site of which was marked by the mound and village
of Khorsabad. It is from the ruins of this edifice
that the splendid collection of Assyrian sculptures
which adorn the galleries of the Louvre have come;
and it is by means of the thorough and systematic
exploration, and the lavish publication of the results
of those works upon this site by the French Government that we gain an insight, such as was little
dreamt would ever be afforded us, into the palace of
an Assyrian king. The work of the French explorers
commenced on this site in 1843 with some slight
private excavations on the part of M. Botta, the
French consul at Mosul, and so much interest was
excited by the discoveries, that almost uninter-

ruptedly from that time until 1855 the work was continued by the French. Not only was the work of exploration carried on, but competent artists and architects were employed to draw the sculptures and plan the buildings unearthed, and the results of their labours were made public in those splendid works, the Monuments de Ninive of M. Botta, and Ninive et L'Assyrie of M. Place, all of which were printed at government expense.

In selecting the palace at Khorsabad as the typical example in our study of Assyrian palaces in general, we have a considerable advantage. In the first place, we are dealing with a palace the work of which is all of one period, and therefore no difficulties arise as to the relative dates of certain portions of the work. In the study, again, of the architecture and plan of the edifice, we have, as M. Perrot has remarked, a great advantage, as in the construction of the royal residence of Sargon the architect was unfettered by any arrangements as to older edifices upon the spot, and was enabled, upon a perfectly new and unencumbered site, to work out to the fullest extent that plan which he had designed. Sargon came to the throne in the year B.C. 722, and died in B.C. 705, his reign lasting therefore seventeen years. From the examination of the ruins at Korsabad it is evident that this suburban palace must have been commenced early in his reign, if not immediately after his succession. If we estimate that twelve years were occupied in the construction of this palace, we are astonished at the stupendous character of the undertaking. The most prominent feature which distinguishes the royal residences of Assyria and Chaldea from those of Egypt, is the large artificial mound upon which they are raised above the level of the surrounding plain. This construction, which forms a sub-basement or pedestal, raises the edifices from 30 to 50 feet above the level of the surrounding plain. It has been customary among some archæologists to regard this mode of building, together with the extensive employment of brick in lieu of stone, as a blind copying on the part of the Assyrians of the style of Chaldea. To this I must dissent; the reason seeming to me to be easily explained on local grounds. The majority of Assyrian palaces—Khorsabad being no exception, for it is near the bank of the Khorsu—are built near to the river and on low ground, and it was necessary, both for protection from the floods and from the attacks of the enemy, to raise the edifices above the level of the surrounding plain. Some idea of the enormous labour employed in the construction of the raised platform alone on which the palace at Khorsabad is built, can be gained when its dimensions are stated. The mound is in the state of a letter T—the stem being somewhat smaller than the cross bar, and projecting a short distance beyond the line of the city ramparts. The palace mound has an area altogether of 25 acres—an area about six times the size of Trafalgar Square. This vast platform is raised 46 feet above the level of the plain. It should be remembered that the whole of the mass is of artificial construction, being composed of sun-dried bricks, faced with kiln-burnt bricks and stone, every fragment of which had to be carried to its place by manual labour. To estimate in some measure the amount of labour, we may remember that the law courts, a block of buildings about one-fourth of the palace at Khorsabad, and standing on no such solid artificial foundation, and in the construction of which the builders were aided by every kind of mechanical appliance, occupied ten years in construction, while, as we know from the tablets, this Assyrian palace did not take so long a time. An examination of the plan of this edifice shows that the architect was guided in his plan by those conditions of oriental life which were the same twenty-six centuries ago in Nineveh as at the present day, and the eye at once divides the complex edifice into the three component elements of an eastern house. On one side we have the royal kingly apartments proper, corresponding to the Seraglio of the houses of India, Persia, and Turkey; adjacent to this was the women's quarter, the Harem; and the third portion, consisting of the stables, offices, and servants' quarters, corresponding to the Khan.

As Mr Perrot remarks, the method adopted by the architect in the arrangements of the three component

parts of the palace is most simple. The whole building is arranged on the rectangular block system, each
department being a separate block. These groups of
chambers, each with a central courtyard, are so
arranged as to touch each other at the angle, or by the
length of side; but they never penetrate into each
other, and never command one another. The excavated portions of the Sennacherib palace at the
south-east end of the Koyunjik mound reveal the
same arrangement of plan, as do also the chambers
in the north-west palace at Nimroud. In Babylonia
we find a similar system of ground-plan in use in the
great temple at Aboo Hubba, where the sacred and
secular portions of the temple are arranged in
separate quadrangles, all grouped round a central
courtyard. Of the external portions of these Assyrian
palaces the most important features were the great
entrance gateways. The principal entrance to the
palace at Khorsabad seems to have been at H;
and, guided by the remains in this quarter, Mr
Thomas, in his restoration, has placed here an
inclined roadway leading into the plain. It will be
observed that this entrance opens directly into the
seraglio or royal quarter. A second entrance was on
the south-west face, and gave admission to court A.
This must have been one of the most magnificent
of Royal gateways. The gateway was 26 feet wide,
and flanked on the outside by six pairs of huge
winged bulls, and two gigantic figures of the great

Chaldean-Assyrian hero Gizdhubar. Some idea of
the constant flow of people, soldiers, servants, and
others, as well as the royal personages who entered
by this lordly portal, is to be gained by the fact that
the pavement was found to be polished and worn by
the tread of many feet. Entering the courtyard A
by this doorway, we cross to the other side, and enter
the royal apartments. It consists of a block of
buildings 200 feet broad by 336 feet long, and contains ten courtyards and sixty chambers. An examination of this section of the building enables us to
divide this department into two parts—the state
rooms, where grand receptions similar to the durbars
of India were held, and which constituted the
salamlik or reception rooms; and the private rooms
of the king. The state rooms are grouped together
round courts I J K L, and all are richly decorated
with sculptures. The heart of this section is formed
by court I, from which six doorways lead into the
various chambers. This court is one of the most
splendid portions of the palace. Four of the six
doorways are flanked by huge winged bulls, and the
walls are decorated with semi-columns of brickwork,
which has been richly coloured, and along the top
ran a cornice of painted brickwork, while a rich
decorative design, in blue and yellow brickwork, ran
over each of the arched doorways. The suggestion
made by M. Perrot, that on state occasions this court
was shaded with coloured awnings, and carpeted with

rich stuffs, and thus converted into a splendid reception room, is very probable.   How glorious must the
scene have been here some twenty-six centuries ago,
where now all is silent as the grave.   What a
mingling of nations, what a babel of tongues must
have greeted the eye and ear on entering this court
on the day when "Sargon, the king of nations,
received the homage of his people."   Swarthy, hardy
soldiers, bronzed by long campaigns in Syria or the
Egyptian frontier; proud, haughty Babylonian priests,
still nurturing deep down in their hearts their schemes
for the restoration of Merodach-baladan, the popular
prince of the Chaldeans ; Chaldeans from the marshes
where the Tigris and Euphrates entered the sea, still
retaining the sharp olive eyes, and high cheek bones
of the Akkadian, stood side by side with their
Elamite and Kassite cousins.   Jews from Jerusalem,
Samaritans from Samaria, rich merchant princes from
Tyre and Sidon, and fair-haired Greeks from the
distant western isles of Yatnan or Cyprus, stood in
picturesque groups awaiting the coming of Assyria's
king.   The long corridor, with its six doorways, each
flanked by winged bulls, must have presented a
magnificent architectural vista when lit with the rays
of the eastern sun, the monotony of light being broken
here and there by rich coloured awnings, which
tinged the sculptured walls.   Leaving the central
court I by the doorway No. 2, we enter the private
apartments of the king, which though not so richly

decorated as the state rooms, are nevertheless ornamented in a delicate style with painted bricks and
stucco work. The chambers grouped round M^1, M^2,
N O P form this section of the royal quarters. Here
we find the living rooms and sleeping chamber of the
king, the latter with a guard room leading into it,
for then, as now, " uneasy lay the head that wore a
crown ;" while the other chambers were the dwellings
of the chief officers and personal attendants of the
king—his scribe or recorder, the abrakku or "lord
chancellor," his priest-augur, astronomers, sword,
bow, and dagger-bearers, his charioteer, and many
other officials ; and looking at the extent of this
portion, covering over 6000 square yards, we see how
large must have been the royal personnel. Ctesias
states that 15,000 officials and domestics were accom-
modated in the palace of the king of Persia. Looking
at the number of chambers here, and remembering
the little that meets the requirements of Indian and
Turkish servants of oriental potentates, we may well
imagine that the estimate of the Greek writer was
not so very exhorbitant. We now come to the large
group of chambers round court I, and a mere examination of the plan shows that the architect has
exercised very considerable ingenuity in the arrangement of his chambers. In the first place, it is to be
noticed that there is no external entrance into this
block, there being only two gateways, and both of
these communicate with the central court A, and are

of peculiar construction. The first entrance at gateway M leads into a square chamber, evidently a guard chamber, and from this a passage at right angles gives entrance into the courtyard; so by this arrangement it is impossible for those on the more public part of the palace to see into this section, or for those within to see outward. The second entrance is protected by double guard-rooms, which lead into a large courtyard (No. 1). From this court, on the right hand, another doorway leads into a quadrangle (No. 2). The court is evidently the central feature of this edifice. From the way in which the court-yards and chambers of this block are arranged, and their careful seclusion from the other parts of the palace, it is evident that this block is the harem quarter of the palace; and this conjecture is confirmed by an inscription found within its precincts, in which the king " prays the gods to render fruitful the royal alliances." The harem in the Assyrian palaces had two names—the first, that which we find applied to the harem palace built by Assurbanipal at Nineveh was Bit-Riduti,—" the house of offspring ;" the other, the same as that applied to the holy of holies of the temple, Parakku—" the forbidden part," " the most sacred part." As I have already remarked, there was a great resemblance between the changes which this word underwent in the Assyrian inscriptions and those varied meanings applied to the Arabic word haram. The central courtyard (No. 2) was the most richly decorated part of the palace. The three principal doors were flanked by collossal sculptures, and by tall standards of bronze, decorated with palm-leaf fans. Before leaving this court, there are three important chambers to be noticed. It will be observed that at three of the angles of the square are chambers (D^1, D^2, D^3) similar in plan. The rooms are long and narrow. About one third of the chamber from the far end is occupied by a raised platform or dais, 2 feet above the rest of the room, and approached by five brick steps, and in the centre of the end wall there is an arched alcove, to which this dais leads. This recess is about 3 feet deep, and the back is ornamented by lines of ornamental brickwork. In this alcove is a broad ottoman or divan about 9 feet long and 3 feet wide. The chamber is ornamented by a friese of coloured and painted bricks running round the walls and over the arch of this recess. It requires but a slight inspection to see that these chambers were three bed chambers. The beds of the Assyrians were probably like those of the Turks and Arabs, quilted mattresses, which were spread out on divans, such as we have here, or on the floor, as the Assyrian *ersu*, bed, is derived, as Dr Delitzsch (Heb. and Assyr., p. 47) has shown, from the root *eresu*, which is a synonym of *rapadu*, "to spread out," as the Arab word for these beds, *firash*, is from *farsh*, "to spread a carpet;" the words *rabitsu* and *mailu* being applied rather to the

couches, such as are figured on the monuments
(B.M., A.B., No. 121). These chambers, of which there
are three, one corresponding to each of the queen's
establishments within the harem quarter (A B C), are
no doubt the same as the king's house referred to in
the book of Esther (ch. ii. 13); while the expression,
" before the court of the women's house " (ch. ii. 11),
is no doubt amply explained by the guarded position
of the outer harem court. Mordecai would therefore
have had to remain in the outer and central court,
and be obliged to obtain his information regarding
Esther from the eunuch guard. It is plainly to be
seen that the harem quarter consisted of three distinct
establishments (A B C), all similar in construction,
though one is somewhat larger than the others, and
was, no doubt, the residence of that important personage, the first wife. The construction of these
establishments is very simple, and each is a complete
and separate house. Taking the larger one as an
example, we have first a paved courtyard, E, in
which a body-guard of eunuchs was stationed. The
central chamber, F, was the living room, in which
the queen spent her time in company with her maids
and attendants, retiring at night to the sleeping
chamber, G, in which we see a similar alcove bed as
in the royal bed-chambers (D^1, D^2, D^3). The small
side chamber, H, was the waiting-room in which
the servants remained, to be within easy call of their
mistress. The long narrow court or passages in A and

B are probably either corridors for exercise, or, as I
am more inclined to think, gardens such as we see
figured in one of the sculptures from Koyunjik (B.M.,
A.B., No. 121). In his arrangement of these establishments it is evident that the royal architect has
been mindful so to isolate each of the residences as
to prevent any quarrels or deeds of vengeance such
as polygamous oriental life often affords examples.
The chambers on the bar of the first courtyard are,
no doubt, as shown by the explorations, the offices of
the harem quarter. Here were found traces of ovens,
large amphoræ which once held wine, and bronze
pots, &c., of the cooking establishment. It is evident
that in this section of the palace we have the royal
residence of the three queens of Sargon, with their
attendant women.

Although the palace of Assurbanipal, on the north
end of the Koyunjik mound, is called by him the
" Harem palace," it exhibits no such arrangement as
that of Sargon at Khorsabad. But it must be remembered that in the English excavations but little
attention has been paid to archæological and architectural details as in the French works, and therefore
in the majority of cases we are quite dependent for
our plans, &c., upon an explorer who has had no
technical training. In this latter place less than
twenty chambers have been explored, and at Khorsabad over 300 have been laid open, carefully planned,
and every detail likely to throw light upon their use

noted down. It is to be hoped that some day the English excavations in Assyria and Babylonia will have that thorough character both in work and necessary appliances which has made the work of Dr Schliemann at Hissarlik, and of Professor Curtius and his assistants, so successful in restoring to us the life of byegone times.

The third section of the palaces, that devoted to the stores, the quarters of the royal guards, the stables of the horses, camels, and other animals, was situated on the south-west and north-west sides of the great quadrangle of the palace (General Plan).

In his annals Sargon thus speaks of his palace, and especially of this section, the *bit nizirte* or " store house," or *bit kamuti* or " treasure house ":—" This palace contains gold, silver, vases of gold and silver, precious stones, copper and iron—the product of rich mines, blue and purple stuff, woven cloth and cotton, amber, ivory, pearls, sandal ebony, horses from Egypt, oxen, donkeys, mules, camels," &c. Of this section of the palace also Esarhaddon, in his cylinder, speaks thus:—" On the left hand of the building (S.E.), in the first month, all the war-horses, mules, asses, camels, arms, furniture of war, all the army, the spoil of my enemies, yearly a regular sum I appointed to be (placed) within it" (W.A.I., vol i., pl. 47, col. vi., lines 46-51). The palace built by Sargon, when compared with those of the middle Assyrian empire at Nimroud, exhibits several new departures in architecture. The arrangement of the rooms, the isolation of the harem, and the offices, show that the art of planning edifices, which I noticed in my previous lecture on the temple had attained considerable perfection at a very early period, had now reached a still higher stage of development. Indeed the palace of Khorsabad, as exhibited to us in the plan prepared by the French explorers, is the only edifice that admits of systematic study. In his inscription, Sargon states that his palace was built *Bit khilanni ina tansil (tamsil) hekal mat khatti*— "A strong house in the style of a Syrian palace" I built. In the inscription known as the Paves des Portes (Botta, pl. 8) the king thus speaks of his palace :—

1. At the foot of the mountain of Muzri (the hills to northeast), over against the city of Nineveh,
2. In the desire of my heart a city I made, and Dur Sargina I proclaimed its name.
3. A palace of ivory, of strong wood and serviceable woods— tamansh, cedar, cyprus and fir, *samli* and *butni*,
4. For the dwelling-place of my majesty, within it I made.
5. Assur the great lord, and the gods inhabiting Assyria, within them I invoked.
6. Victims, noble sacrifices, before them I offered.
7. Of the kings of the four quarters who to the yoke of my lordship had submitted,
8. From the prefects of my land, with the wise men, scribes, and princes,
9. The officers and scribes, their rich offerings I received.
10. Within it I caused them to dwell, and I established joy.

The next palace we have to consider is that of Assurbanipal, on the north end of the Koyunjik

mound, which was discovered by Mr Hormuzd
Rassam in 1854. This palace must have been built
about B.C. 650—about sixty or seventy years after
the palace of Khorsabad. It is impossible to apply
the detailed treatment to this palace which we have
given to that of Sargon, but from an art point of
view this edifice is more important. Entering by the
western portal, a porch 23 feet wide, we at once meet
with an innovation in Assyrian architecture. The
wide expanse of doorway is broken by two columns,
which have hitherto found no place in Assyrian
architecture. This portal gives entrance into a large
hall or vestibule (55 feet by 20 feet), and immediately
opposite the doorway is a large guard-chamber, with
an inner chamber for the captain of the guard.
Turning to the right, we enter a small hall, and
passing through this we come to a long inclined
passage leading up to the level of the palace platform.
This passage has been lined with sculptures representing the grooms leading horses, and the attendants
bringing game, fruits, &c., as offerings to the palace
—stone counterparts of the living who day by day
in the byegone past ascended this entrance to the
abode of royalty. At the distance of 175 feet
this corridor turns to the right, and leads up to
a large hall, the doorway of which is also sub-
divided by columns. A doorway on the right
leads into an open courtyard (54 × 43). Crossing
this courtyard we enter a long narrow gallery

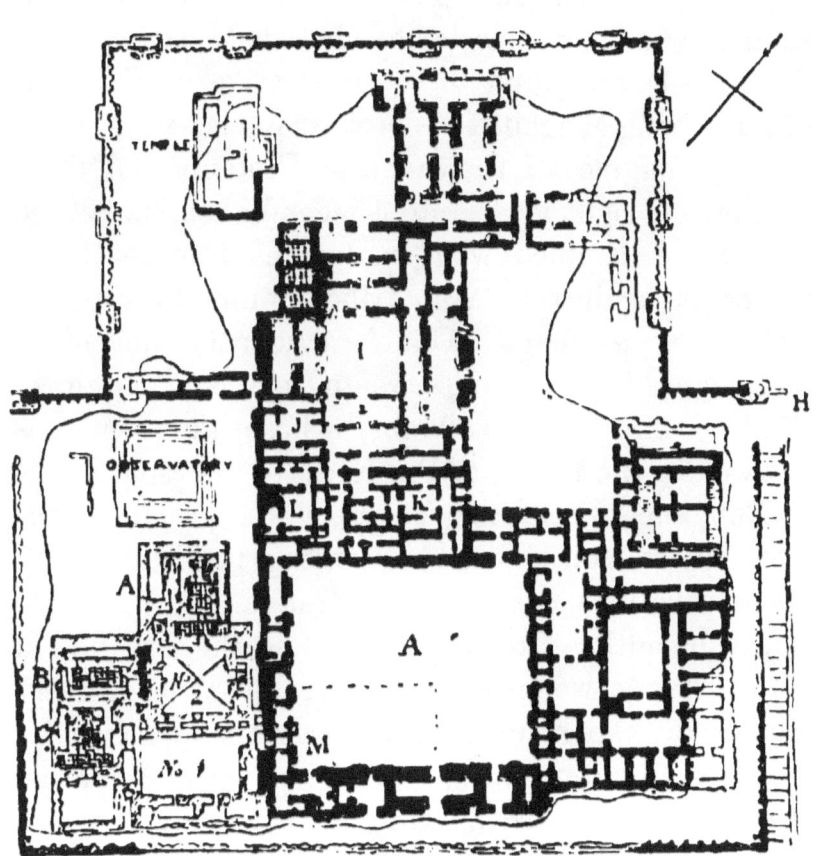

Palace of Sargon.

(112 × 38), the walls of which were lined with sculptures, and with plain marble slabs awaiting the sculptor's chisel. The sculptures found here, some of which are now in the British Museum (B.M., A.B., 91-4), are found to be illustrative of the wars of Assurbanipal against his brother Samas-suma-ukin, the Saulmugines of the canon of Plotemy. A door-way on the right leads into a second chamber (60 × 21), which is lined with sculptures representing a campaign against an Arab tribe, mounted on camels and living in tents. This is evidently the ninth campaign of this king's reign against Vaiteh or Watieh, king of the Arabs, whose kingdom was situated in the region of the Nedj, to the south-west of Babylon. From this chamber we pass into the great central court, which, according to Mr Rassam's test excavations, measured 155 feet in length, by 125 feet in breadth. Crossing to the north-west side of the courtyard, we enter by a broad portico (43 feet), broken in like manner to the western entrance by columns, an outer hall (70 × 22), leading into another broad corridor. Passing through this hall we enter a small square room (20 × 20), two sides of which are pannelled with sculptured slabs representing the wars of Assurbanipal against the Elamites. The majority of these sculptures, in good preservation, have been removed to the British Museum (B.M., A.B., No. 54-62).

Leaving this part of the palace, we return to the

end of the ascending passage, and find facing us a long narrow gallery, lined on either side with the finest examples of Assyrian art. This gallery (12 × 57) is decorated with a series of sculptures illustrative of the exploits of the king in the hunting field.

We have now completed the tour of the chief rooms of this explored portion of the royal palace, and one or two important variations from the structure and decoration of the palace of Sargon at Khorsabad are to be noticed. In the first place, several of the rooms are larger than those at Khorsabad, and the arrangement with regard to each other is by no means so systematic, there being no trace of that series of complete blocks which made the former so perfect a plan. As an example of this, I may point to the almost complete seclusion of the Susianian room, and the manifest variation of the plan from those of the palaces of Sennacherib, Sargon, or the kings of the middle empire. A still more striking innovation is the introduction of columns in the principal doorways. As this palace was erected shortly after the king's victorious campaigns in Egypt, which culminated in the capture of Thebes and Memphis, the introduction of these columned portals may be due to foreign influence. In the account of his spoilation of Thebes, the Assyrian king states that he brought from there " two great obelisks of polished granite, of which their weight was 2500 talents. Standing before the gate of a temple, from

their position I removed them, and to Assyria
conducted them" (Cylinder, Rm. i., col. ii., 41-43).
These objects were evidently strange to the Assyrian
king, as he applies to them the name *temien*, or
"foundation-stones," a word also applied to the
boundary-stones or land-marks to which the king no
doubt compared them. There must have been very
great difficulty in transporting these objects so far,
their weight being a little over ninety-one tons.
Some idea of the manual labour which the Assyrians
could command is to be gained from the sculptures
in the Koyunjik room representing the building of
Sennacherib's palace, but what must the work have
been of conveying these great monoliths from the
Syrian coast overland to Nineveh!

The palace of Assurbanipal was commenced on the
15th day of the month Iyar (April-May), in the
Eponym year of Assur-danin-ani, the prefect of
Akkad; that would be, according to the Eponym
canon, the year B.C. 640. In the construction of
the palace the king employed the captives and spoil
taken of the Elamite cities, and the captive Arabs
and their kings captured in his Arab wars. This
would place the building of this palace as late as B.C.
650 at least, and account in a great measure for the
unfinished state of several of the chambers and
corridors. Just as the palace of Sargon at Khorsabad
had exceeded all former palaces in the completeness
of its plan, so did this new palace, the last of

Assyria's royal residences, excel all former palaces in the beauty of its sculptured decorations. The stiff conventional work of the middle empire, such as adorned the palaces of Assurnazirpal and Shalmanesar in the city of Calah, had now given place to a more finished style, and the wars and ceremonies of the great king were represented in a series of stone tableaux of the highest artistic merit. This improvement first makes itself apparent in the sculptures from the palace of Sennacherib on the south-east extremity of the Koyunjik mound, which represent the Syrian wars, including the siege of Lachish, and the wars in Babylonia against Merodach-baladan; although perhaps an earlier phase of this development may be seen in the close attention to detail exhibited in the bronze reliefs from the temple at Ballawat. In the historical sculptures from the palace of Assur-nazir-pal (B.C. 885), in the Nimroud gallery of the British Museum (No. 7, 18), we see a series of representations of the wars of this king, the march of the army, the crossing of rivers, the encampment, the siege and surrender of cities; all these incidents are depicted in a regular machine-like manner; no attempt is made to indicate the locality of the cities or campaigns, nor is any attempt made to distinguish the nations against whom the Assyrians are fighting. In the bronze gates from Ballawat we see the first attempts to render these sculptured tableaux really illustrative of the annals of the king. The nature of

the material employed did not admit of any very
great accuracy; but we can see that one city is
distinct from another, and special local features, such
as the spot where the king's statue was carved on the
shores of Lake Van, or at the head waters of the
Subnat, the modern Tebbeneh Su, are represented in
a much more accurate manner. Some distinction,
too, is made between the various races against whom
the king is fighting, as between the people of Uradhi
or Ararat, and the Hittites and Babylonians. In
the sculptures of the time of Sennacherib and his
successors, this idea of rendering the works a series
of folio plates to illustrate the campaigns described
on the cylinders and tablets, and to make them as
accurate in local and ethnic features as possible, is
carried to a very advanced stage. In the wars
against Merodach-baladan we have the thick marshes
of tall reeds which formed the lower portion of the
Tigro-Euphrates delta, the modern Afadj, the land of
Gumbulu or Guzummani of the inscriptions. The
population then bade defiance to the Assyrians, as
at the present time the half-bred Arabs of this
district do to the Turkish pashas of Bagdad, in their
reed islands, darting from one to the other in boats
and rafts. In these sculptures we see the artist
must have studied and endeavoured to reproduce
the local features of the region. The Babylonian
supporters of Merodach-baladan are here represented
as hiding in the islands, or escaping from the Assyrian

soldiers in boats and rafts. On the banks of the rivers, on the more solid ground, are groves of palm trees; the whole being an excellent illustration of the flight of the Babylonian prince, thus described by Sennacherib:—"In the beginning of my reign I accomplished the overthrow of Merodach-baladan, king of Ganduniyas, with the armies of Elam, within the neighbourhood of the city of Kisu (Hymer). In the midst of that battle he forsook his camp, he fled alone, to the country of Guzummani he fled. Among the marshes and pools he descended, and his life thus he saved. I also took the road after him, to the country of Guzummani, my fighting men to the midst of the pools and marshes I urged, and five days they moved about rapidly, but his hiding-place was not seen" (Bellin's Cylinder, 6, 7, and 11). The Babylonians, represented in these sculptures (B.M., K.G., No. 4-8), are distinct in type from the Assyrian soldiers—shorter in statue, with close curly hair, and small eyes, and high cheek bones, as if retaining the type of their Akkadian ancestors. So in like manner in slabs representing campaigns in Palestine (B.M., A.B., 21-32; B.M., K.G., 20-26) is the Jewish, Arab, or Negro face clearly to be distinguished from the Assyrian. Not only has the artist endeavoured to be accurate in details, but he has introduced some incidents into his tableau, such as fishermen on rafts or skins angling in the river, women giving water to their children, or groups of people flying from the enemy, with their household goods on carts—all of these tending to give a far more realistic character to these sculptures than was the case with the work of the artists of the 8th and 9th centuries before our era.

These sculptures so accurately represent the various types of people with whom the Assyrians came in contact, that they are of the highest value for the study of the ethnology of Western Asia. Accurate as the Assyrians were in the representation of these foreign nations, they seem to have been strangely conservative in regard to themselves. From the earliest time down to this period of Assyrian art there is no attempt at portraiture—the same type of face, sometimes with a beard, sometimes beardless, is given indiscriminately to their figures — the differences which exist between one face and another during all this time being due only to the slight modification of style which took place.

Although Assyrian art was so stereotyped in regard to portraiture, it attained a very high perfection in other branches, notably in the representation of animal life; and the highest developement is exhibited in the sculptures from the lion hunt room. So fine are these sculptures, so free from the conventionalties which had hitherto fettered Assyrian art, that some German critics have gone so far as to suggest that Grecian artists were employed on them. Such a competent authority, however, as Mr Poynter,

R.A., very effectively combats this idea by calling attention to the very primitive condition of the arts in Greece during the middle of the seventh century before the Christian era. These sculptures, which now adorn the Assyrian basement of the British Museum, prove that the artists must have studied with close attention the habits of the lion, wild ass, and gazelle, and endeavoured to reproduce them with the utmost fidelity. I may mention such striking examples as the paralysed lion shot through the spine, or a still more perfectly finished group of a lion and lioness, in which the latter is crouching with cat-like playfulness at his feet.

We have now seen how these sculptured tableaux, ranged line after line along the walls of the halls of the royal palaces, formed large plates illustrative of the history of the reigns of the kings whose abodes they adorned.

In this brief account of the royal palaces of Assyria, we learn how little is the change in Oriental life during a long range of centuries. The same groups of state rooms, the secluded and richly decorated harem, and the accommodation for hosts of servants and soldiers, constitute the residence of an eastern sultan or pasha at the present time, as they did twenty-five centuries ago the abode of the lords of Assyria.

CHALDEAN DELUGE LEGEND.

IN entering upon the study of this remarkable inscription, we are bringing our cuneiform records into more direct comparison with Biblical and other ancient writings than was the case when the Creation legends were under consideration. The Deluge legend, in one form or another, is one of the most universal of traditions. Among ancient civilisations we find it in the Chinese legend of Fáh-he, who escaped with his wife, three sons, and daughters, from the universal cataclysm. It forms an episode in the Incarnations of Vishnu, and even the new world has the ancient Astec traditions of this great visitation of divine wrath. In dealing with the manifold traditions which have come from all parts of the world—Europe, Asia, America; Africa alone being exempt,—and from many of the islands of Polynesia, considerable care has to be exercised, as many of the traditions are found so strikingly to resemble the Hebrew account as rather to prejudice their evidence. - As an example of one of these, I may quote a tradition from Borneo :—"There was a great inundation, when the ancestors of the human family of the Chinese, Malays, and Dyaks apparently dwelt together. The three had to swim for their lives, and all came to land safely." This tradition, together with very striking ones of the Tower of Babel, which in Dyak legend is replaced by a big ladder, and others, are found in a paper by Mr Alexander Mackenzie Cameron, and are quoted as striking confirmations of the Hebrew account (Trans. Soc. Bib. Arch., vol. ii., p. 264-5). This is one among many traditions which have come to us from the East, and which are often to be obtained, furnished with miraculous resemblances to the Genesis legend, if the natives are but slightly prompted. I do not therefore, in this lecture, propose to enter a comparison between these legends and the Chaldean account, as contained in the Deluge Tablet. There are, however, among Oriental traditions of this great cataclysm, three which stand out as pre-eminently ancient. The Hebrew accounts in Genesis (chaps. vi.-xi. 8), the versions of the Chaldean tradition preserved in the writings of the Greco-Chaldean historian Berosus, and to these we may now add the more ancient version of the original Chaldean inscription from which Berosus at least derived his account. The story of the discovery of this important inscription, which took place about twelve years ago, by the late

D

Mr George Smith, is well known, but it requires recapitulation, in order that at the outset of our study of this important document we may clearly understand the position this legend holds in the mass of Chaldean literature. The very direct references in the Scriptures (Gen. x. 8-10 ; Micah v. 6) to Nimrod as the great hero of Chaldea, as well as the numerous legends of Hebrew, Arab, and Greek writers, always lead the decipherers to hope that some day there would be revealed, from beneath the dust of centuries the legends which the Chaldeans themselves had of this ancestor of their nation. In 1872 Mr Smith found a number of a series of tablets which related to a hero, who was a mighty-one on earth, bearing the title of "the warrior, perfect in strength," and distinguishing himself in war and in the hunting-field. It was evident, from the descriptions of this hero's great deeds, that he was the same person as that powerful giant god so often represented in the Assyrian sculptures at Khorsabad, and on the engraved cylinder seals. Other fragments of these tablets having been obtained from the East, it was found that the series of tablets when complete consisted of twelve tablet-books, each one corresponding to one of the twelve deeds or labours of this Chaldean Hercules. The hero of this cycle of poems is called Gizdhubar, a name which is of non-Semitic—probably Akkadian — origin, and means the "mass of fire." The epithets applied to him are nearly all solar, as in a hymn addressed to the hero (S. 1877) he is called "Gizdhubar the king, perfect in strength, the judge of the spirits, the exalted prince, the chief of mankind, the watchman of the four quarters, the glory of the earth, the lord of the underworld." All these epithets are applied to the Sun god in other hymns, so that, guided by these facts and by the character of the legends preserved, Sir Henry Rawlinson was able to point out the solar character of the Epic of Chaldea. It is evident, as I shall show in a subsequent lecture, that the stories in this cycle of legends were arranged according to the sun's passage through the signs of the Zodiac. It had long been recognised that the Akkadian calendar was so arranged, many of the months bearing names which pointed to the signs most distinctly. As I treat of this subject more fully in a subsequent lecture, I may only quote these most striking examples. The second tablet contains the story of the half bull-like companion of the hero, who companions him in all his labours, as the centaur Chiron attended Hercules. It corresponds to the second month, called "the month of the directing bull," and the Zodiac sign of Taurus. For the third month we have a story of two twin sisters, Samkhat and Kharimat, who entice this centaur-like companion to come to the court of Gizdhubar, corresponding to the sign of Gemini. For the sixth month, called the "month of message of Istar," we have the sixth tablet, containing the stories

of the love proposals of the goddess to the hero, and
in agreement with the sign of Virgo. Lastly, we
find the eleventh tablet, which, according to this
arrangement should correspond to the " month of the
curse of rain," and to the sign of Aquarius, has
woven into its columns the story of the deluge. It
is therefore clear that the tale of the preservation of
the Chaldean sage—whose name in the tablet is
Samas-napisti, "the Sun of Life," or "the Living
Sun," the Xisuthrus of Berosus, the Noah of the
Hebrew tradition—is here brought into the epic as
an episode to keep it in harmony with the zodiacal
arrangement. We have therefore recovered with the
decipherment of this series of legends the originals of
many of the traditions of Nimrod, but also a far older
legend embodied in the epic, the story of the deluge.
From the preceding tablet, the tenth, we learn that
the hero, sick and afflicted, being covered with leprosy
and deprived of his hair, wherein, like the Hebrew
Samson, lay his strength, is journeying to learn the
secret of immortality. This secret, " the hidden thing
of the gods " as it is here called, can only be revealed
by the ancient sage Samas-napisti, who has been
translated by the gods to dwell as one of themselves
in immortality on an island near the mouth of the
Tigris and Euphrates. To this remote spot he is
guided by the Chaldean Charon, a mythic personage
named Nis-Hea, " the Man of Hea "—that is, the
servant of the water god, of whom I have already

spoken in my lecture on the Creation Tablets, who
pilots him across the river and waters of death to this
land where the translated sage lives. Having reached
the place, the hero speaks to the Chaldean Noah and
lays before him the object of his visit. "Gizdhubar
to him, even Samas-napisti the remote, spake: I am
burdened with a decree. The cure thou repeatest not
to me, even thou—the rest of thy heart from making
tribulation . . . . to thee I am come up. What hast
thou laid hold of in the assembly of the gods where
thou art placed?" The translated sage then proceeds
"to relate the story of his preservation," and the next
173 lines are occupied with an account of the deluge
and the translation of Samas-napisti. There are
many indications that this story is much older
than the complete epic of Gizdhubar; and even in
the tablets the commencement of the story is carefully lined off from the rest of the inscription.
Before passing to the comparative analysis of this
inscription, we may refer to one or two facts bearing
on this historical character which the Chaldeans
have attached to the deluge. One of the strongest
pieces of evidence is to be found in the tablet of
royal names (W.A.I., vol. v., pl. 47), where the important gloss appears—"These are the kings ruling after
the deluge (abubi), who according to their relative
order wrote not." In like manner the story of the
preservation of Sargon, of Agadhe or Akkad, in an
ark of bulrushes on the Euphrates, and his elevation

to the throne, may be a transference of the deluge tradition to this hero of the Semites, whose remote antiquity (3750 B.C.) might cause him to become tinged with a mythic glamour. The deluge formed the rubicon between the mythic period and the heroic and polyarchal age, separating the reigns of local kings from the far distant age of the ten antedeluvian patriarchs. The patriarchs are thus named by Berosus, and the length of their reigns given. They may be compared with the ante-diluvian patriarchs of Genesis—

1. Alorus.........10 Sar.		Adam.
2. Alaparos 3		Seth.
3. Amillaros......13		Enos.
4. Ammenon.....12		Cainan.
5. Amelagaros....18		Mahalālēl.
6. Davos..........10		Jared.
7. Euedoranchos 18		Enoch.
8. Amempsinos 10		Methuselah.
9. Obartus........ 8		Lamech.
10. Xisuthrus......18		Noah.

$$120 \ = \ 432,000 \ \text{years.}$$

The genealogy of the hero of the Deluge is given in the tablet (col. i. 20)—"Oh, man of the city of

Surippak, son of Ubarratutis." This latter is Obartes or Otiartes of Berosus, who was king of Larancha, according to the Greek text, but which M. Lenormant has shown was a corruption of Sorippak (La Langue Primitive, p. 342). The name Xisuthrus, which Berosus gives to the Chaldean Noah, may be a corruption of the epithets Adra Khasis, "Reverent and Holy," applied to the hero in col. i. 45, and in col. iv. 22; but it is hardly possible—the more likely solution being that it is a Hellenicised form of Zi-Susru, "the Spirit of the Founder," and perhaps such an etymology may explain the translation of Xisuthrus, recorded by Berosus—"They remaining within (the ark), finding their companions, did not return, quitted the vessel with many lamentations, calling continually on the name of Xisuthrus. Him they saw no more; but they could distinguish his voice in the air, and hear him admonish them to pay due regard to religion." The city of Surrippak, of which Samas Napisti or Xisuthrus was king, is called "the Ship City" (W. A. I., ii. 46, 1), and the Lord of the city was the god Hea—the god of rivers, seas, and ships —who takes so prominent a part in this legend in protecting the sage. He is here called "the Lord of Ships—Hea, the Lord of Surippak" (W. A. I., ii. 60, 21). The city was an ancient one long prior to the time of the king Khammurabi, B.C. 2120, who records its capture. It was probably situated below Ur and Erech, the modern Mughier, and Warka, and near the mouth of the Euphrates, which, in ancient times, as late as the reign of Sennacherib, entered the Persian Gulf by a separate mouth from the Tigris —the name of the father of the Chaldean Noah, Ubara-Tutu—the name being explained in the syllabaries and bilingual tablets as Ubarra = *Kidinu*- "Servant" (W. A. I., ii., pl. 3, No 254); and the god Tutu is given in the bilingual list of royal names as the synonym of Marduk or Merodach (W. A. I., v 42, 18). In a bilingual tablet (K. 2107), the god Tutu is called *Muallad ili Mūddis ili*—"the generator and restorer of the gods"—in which character he may be identified with Merodach as the god of the dawn and twilight. In this relationship Samas-Napisti, "the Living Sun," would be the child of the "Servant of the Dawns," as this name means—rising each day at his message, and setting each day by his decree.

CHALDEAN DELUGE TABLET.

COL. I.

The first eight lines of the inscription are introductory matter, being a conversation between Gizdhubar and Samas-Napisti—the Chaldean Noah.

Samas-Napisti then commences to relate the story of his preservation from the " great flood."

Line   9 Let me reveal to thee, Oh ! Gizdhubar, the story of my preservation

     10 And the hidden thing of the gods let me tell to thee

11 The city of Surippak, which thou knowest is placed
    on the Euphrates

12 That city was very ancient (when) the gods within it

13 [Were not honored, I only was] the servant of the
    great gods

14 Their father Anu their king ; their

15 Counsellor the warrior Bel ; their

16 Throne-bearer the god Adar, and

17 The god Hea, the Lord of the underworld

18 Repeated their decree

19 I this destiny hearing (as) he said to me

20 Oh ! Man of Surippak, son of Ubarratutu

21 Destroy the house and build a ship

22 For I will destroy the seed and the life

23 Cause them to go up into the ship all seed that hath
    life

24-25 The ship which thou shalt make—cubits its length in
    measure

26 —cubits the contents of its breadth and height

27   above the deep roof it over

28 I understood, and said to Hea, my Lord

29 The building of the ship which thou commandedest

30 If it be made by me

31 Then will laugh at me, the children of the people,
    and the old men

32 Hea opened his mouth and spake to me, his servant

33 If they laugh at thee, thou shalt say to them

34 Every one who has turned from me

35 Shall be punished, for the protection of the gods is
    over me

36

37 I will judge my judgment upon all above and below

38 Close not the ship

39 Until the season, when I shall send thee word
    (saying)

40 " Enter the ship and close the door "

41 In the interior of it, thy grain, thy furniture, thy goods

42 Thy wealth, thy man-servants and maid-servants, and thy young men

43 The cattle of the field and the animals of the field As many as I would preserve

44 I will send to thee, (then) make firm thy door

45 The Reverent and Holy One opened his mouth and spake to Hea, his Lord

46 No one has made such a ship

47   on the ground (to hold all things)

48 [The form of] the ship let me see

49 And on the ground I will make the ship which thou commandest

Col. II

Line 2 On the fifth day two sides were raised

3 In its enclosure (hull) fourteen ribs

4 Also fourteen they numbered above

5 I placed its roof and enclosed it

6 Sixthly I made it firm, seventhly I divided its passages

7 Eightly its interior I examined

8 Openings to the waters I stopped

9 I searched for cracks and the wanting parts I fixed

10 Three *sari* of bitumen I poured over the outside

11 Three *sari* of bitumen I poured over the interior

12 Three *sari* of men bearers who carried chests on their heads

13 I kept a *saros* of chests for my people to eat

14 Two *sari* of chests I divided among the boatmen

15 To the gods I caused oxen to be scarified

16 I appointed the portions for each day

17   and wine

18 I gathered like the waters of the river

19 And food as the dust of the earth
20 In receptacles my hand placed
21 With the help of the Sun god, the ship was completed
22 All was made strong and—
23 And above and below the tackling was fixed
24 Then of my possessions I took two-thirds
25 All I had of silver I gathered together
26 All I had of gold I gathered together
27 All I had of the seed of life I gathered together the whole
28 I caused them all to go up into the ship. All my men-servants and maid-servants
29 The cattle of the field and the beast of the field and the young men, all of them, I caused to go up
30 The season the Sun god had fixed, and (of which) he spake saying
31 "I will cause it to rain from heaven heavily"
32 "Enter into the midst of the ship and close thy door"
33 (That) season fixed came round (of which)
34 He spake saying; "I will cause it to rain from heaven heavily"
35 Of that day when I reached the twilight
36 The day which I had watched for with fear
37 I entered into my ship and closed my door
38 That I might close my ship to Bazur Sadai-rabu
39 The boatman, the great-house, I gave with all its goods
40 Then rose the water of dawn at daylight
41 Like a black cloud on the horizon of heaven
42 The thunder god in the midst of it thundered
43 Nebo and the Wind god march in front
44 The throne bearers (storm clouds) go o'er mountain and plain
45 The Pestilence god brings with him affliction
46 The War god goes in front and casts down
47 The angels of earth carry the destruction

48 In their glory they swept through the land
49 The deluge of the Rain god reaches to heaven
50 The darkened earth to waste is turned

Col. III.

Line 1 The surface of the earth like fire they sweep
      2 They destroyed all life from the face of the earth
      3 To battle against men they brought the deluge
      4 Brother saw not brother, men knew one another
      5 Even in heaven the gods feared the flood
      6 And sought refuge, they ascended to the heaven of
        Anu
      7 The gods like dogs in kennels lay in heaps
      8 Then cried I star like a mother
      9 And the great goddess does utter her speech
     10 All things to clay are turned
     11 And the evil which I proclaimed in the presence of
        the gods
     12 As I announced in the presence of the gods, is that
        evil
     13 As I announced to evil are devoted all my people
     14 And though I the mother have begotten my people
     15 Yet like the spawn of fishes they fill the sea
     16 Then the gods were weeping with her concerning the
        spirits
     17 The gods on the throne were seated weeping
     18 Covered were their lips because of the coming evil
     19 Six days and nights
     20 The wind, the deluge and the storm go on sweeping
        away
     21 The seventh day when it approached the rain sub-
        sided, and the great deluge
     22 Which had assailed like a host
     23 Was appeased.   The sea began to dry and the wind
        and flood ended
     24 I watched the sea making a tossing

25 And the whole of mankind had turned to clay

26 Like reeds the corpses floated

27 I opened the window and the light struck on my face

28 I was sad at heart, I sat down, I wept

29 Over my face flowed my tears

30 I looked at the regions bounding the sea

31 To the 12 points no land (was seen)

32 To the country of Nizir floated the ship

33 The mountain of Nizir stopped the ship and to pass o'er it was not able

34 The first day, the second day the M. Nizir the same

35 The third day and fourth day the M. Nizir the same

36 The fifth and sixth day the M. Nizir the same

37 On the seventh day in the course of it

38 I sent forth a dove, it left. The dove went and turned

39 A resting place it saw not, it returned back

40 I sent forth a swallow, it left and turned and

41 A resting place it could not see, and it returned back

42 I sent forth a raven and it left

43 The raven went and the corpses (carrion) which were on the water it saw

44 It did eat—it floated and was carried away—it returned not

45 I sent the (animals) forth to the four winds (of heaven) I sacrificed a sacrifice

46 I built the altar on the peak of the mountain

47 Adgur jars by sevens I placed

48 Below them I spread reeds, pine wood and spices

49 The gods smelled the odour. The gods smelled the sweet odour

50 The gods like flies over the master the sacrifice gathered

51 Then from afar the great goddess in her approach

52 Raised up the great zones which Ann had created as his glory

COL. IV.

Line 1 Those days I had thought of and never may I forget
them

2 May the gods come to my altar ;

3 May Bel not come to my altar

4 Since he did not reflect and made a deluge

5 And consigned my people to the deep

6 When thereupon Bel in his approach

7 Saw the ship stopped. His heart was filled with
anger upon gods and spirits

8 Let none come forth alive. Let no man escape the
deep

9 Adar opened his mouth and spake, he says to the
warrior Bel

10 Whosoever except Hea can make a design

11 Even Hea knows and all things he teaches

12 Hea opened his mouth and spake, he says to the
warrior Bel

13–14 Oh ! thou counsellor of the gods, why, why didst
thou reflect and didst make a deluge

15 Let the doer of sin bear his sin and let the trans-
gressor bear his transgression

16 May the just prince not be cut off, may the faithful
not perish

17 Instead of making a deluge, may lions increase and
men be decreased

18 Instead of making a deluge, may jackals increase
and men be decreased

19 Instead of making a deluge, may famine happen and
men be wasted

20 Instead of making a deluge, may pestilence increase
and men decrease

21 I did not reveal the hidden thing of the gods

22 To the Reverent and Holy One a dream I sent him
and the hidden thing he heard

23 When Bel had reflect on his counsel he went up into
the midst of the ship

24 He took my hand and raised me up

25 He caused me to rise up and placed my wife by my
side

26 He turned himself to us and established himself to
us in a covenant

27 Hitherto Samas-Napisti has been a mortal man

28 Even now Samas-Napisti and his wife are raised up
and borne away as gods

29 Then shall dwell Samas-Napisti in a remote place at
the mouth of the rivers

30 They took us, and in a remote place at the mouth of
the rivers they seated us

At the commencement of the tablet we have an
account of the council of the gods over the wicked-
ness of the people, especially those of the city of
Xisuthrus. The words here furnish an almost direct
parallel to the Hebrew, omitting, of course, the
polytheistic elements of the Chaldean version : " That
city was very ancient, when the gods within it (were
not honoured); I only was the servant of the great
gods "—to which we may compare the following
passages : " But Noah found grace in the eyes of the
Lord. And Noah was a just man, and perfect in his
generations, and Noah walked with God " (Gen. vi.
8, 9). And both the Hebrew and Chaldean accounts
are in agreement as to the cataclysm being a punishment for sin. There are other records among the
Assyrian inscriptions of punishments sent upon men
by the gods, and in every case the infliction seems to

be by decision of a council of the gods. In the legend of Atarpi, where drought famine is the punishment, the gods decide to punish men; so in the Dibbara legends, where pestilence is the instrument of divine wrath, is there a council of the gods. In this Olympian congress we find the members of the great Chaldean trinity, Anu, Bel, and Hea, taking part. Anu, "the Father," the Dyaus-pitar or Jupiter, being at the head. It is Bel, the lord of mundane affairs, who seems to be the offended one among the gods, and it is against him that the people had sinned. He is here called *Malik Sunu*, "their counsellor," and advises that the punishment shall be by a terrible deluge—and "the seed and the life" were all to be destroyed; "let none escape the deep —all were consigned to the deep." Hea, the third member of the triad, "the lord of wisdom," who appears here as Hermes, the herald of the gods, acts as the saviour of the few just persons among the sinners. Sir Henry Rawlinson has suggested, and with very good reasons, that there was in Chaldea a sect who worshipped Hea as their supreme god, and who approached very near to a monotheistic creed. From the prominence given to this god in the Deluge Tablet, it would seem as if this was a document of that school of Chaldean thought. Hea was, as I have shown, the Lord of Surippak, the city of Samas-Napisti, or Xisuthrus, who always addresses him as "Hea, my Lord" (Col. i. 28-45), and from whom he receives instructions in building the ark or ship (Col. i. 21 49). The mediatorial office he assumes with the enraged god Bel (Col. iv., 12-22) would mark him as the special protector of this people. The instructions which Hea gives as to the building of the vessel in which Samas-Napisti is to be saved are most precise, and are very important in the consideration of the relation of that story to those of the Hebrews. The vessel to be built was a ship *elapu*, provided with "hull with fourteen ribs on either side," "a roof," by which here I suspect the deck is meant as closing in the hull; this latter portion being divided into sections. "I divided its passages" (Sukut), literally "streets," and the whole covered without and within with a coat of bitumen, and provided with ropes or tackling above and below. This points clearly to a ship of some size, and to a knowledge of ship-building. That ship-building was known in Chaldea at an early time is shown by the reference to ships in some of the most ancient hymns, especially in a difficult tablet (W. A. I. iv. 25, col. i.); and a legendary fragment, which Mr George Smith at one time included in the Gizdhubar series (K. 3200), speaks of ships coming up the Euphrates as far as Erech, the modern Warka—that is about 120 miles above Kurna, where the rivers now join. But we are not confined merely to legendary evidence, for in the inscription of Gudea, found at Tello on the Shat el Hie, this king, who reigned at least as early as B.C. 2500, speaks of sending ships from the Persian

Gulf to the land of Magan, which is now almost universally identified by Assyriologists as the Sinaitic peninsula, to obtain the stones, diorite, and porphyry for his royal statues. Ships from the Red Sea also came to Chaldea, as the ships of Magan are mentioned in a list of vessels. An important bilingual tablet (W. A. I. i., ii., 62, No. 2) gives the names of several kinds of ships and their various parts. We have " the ship" and vessels carrying as much tonnage as 60 or 90 gur. We have also the " ferry boat," called *nibiree* or " the crossing boat," and the *makhirtuv* or " market boat ;" also the names of many parts of the ship. The keel is called " the foundation of the ship," the deck " the ground of the ship," the bow and stern " the horns of the ship," and the ribs " the sides." There was a deck-house also, which explains the passage in this Deluge tablet : " To Buzur-sadai-rabu, the boatmen, the *great house* (*ekal*) I gave with all its goods." As this ship exceeded all others in size, so its deck-house was a palace to all other deck-houses. The prow of the ship was called " the eye " or face of the ship, reminding us of the Chinese custom of painting eyes on the prow of the junks. In this tablet we have a list of the sacred arks or barges of the gods, and that of Hea is called " the ship of the lord ruler of the Absi ;" while that of his wife Bahu, whom I have already referred to in the lecture on the Creation legends, is called " the ship of the noble lady ;" that of the moon " the ship of light," while that of his consort, the evening star, is called "the ship of the lesser light;" that of Merodach "the oracle ship," and of Bel "the ship of the world." From these inscriptions, many of which are either in or accompanied by the Akkadian versions of the texts, we see that the ancient inhabitants of Chaldea had attained some considerable knowledge of ship-building at a very remote period, and therefore gave to their Deluge legend a more nautical character than did the Hebrews. The word used in our authorised version, ark, is simply the rendering of the word *tebah*, a box or chest. The same word is applied to the basket in which Moses was exposed on the Nile (En. ii. 3), which the LXX renders by *kibotos*, and the Vulgate by *Arca*. The ark of Noah was to be built of gopher wood, and, like that of Xisuthrus, to be coated with pitch without and within. It was also to have a roof—the reading of our version (Gen. vi. 16) being better amended to "a roof," according to Ewald and Schultze,—also doors and windows ; but there is nothing in the description which can identify the construction described as a ship.

We come now to the provisioning of the ark, which in the Chaldean account is much more detailed than in the Hebrew. In the Book of Genesis we have two versions of this—the first usually called the Elohistic (Gen. vi. 18-2): " Thou shalt come into the ark, thou, and thy sons, and thy wife, and thy sons' wives. And of every living thing of all flesh, two of every sort shalt thou bring into the ark, to keep *them* alive; they shall be male and female. Of fowls after their kind, of cattle after their kind, and of every creeping thing of the earth after his kind, two of every sort shall come unto thee, to keep them alive. And take thou unto thee all food that is eaten, and thou shalt gather it unto thee; and it shall be for thee and for them. Thus did Noah, according to all that God (Elohim) had commanded him to do." In the next chapter (vii. 2-3) the instructions are repeated, but the selected animals are to be only those of the clean kind, and these are to be selected by sevens. The phraseology of the first account recalls to our minds the words of the seventh creation fragment, in which the cattle and creeping things are so emphatically specified, and resembles the tablet more clearly than the second: "Enter into the ship, and close the door. In the interior of it, thy grain, thy furniture, thy goods, thy wealth, thy man-servants and maid-servants, thy young men, the cattle of the field and animals of the field, as many as I would preserve I will send to thee" (Col. i. 40-44). Here no distinction is made as to clean or unclean animals— the latter no doubt being intended for the sacrifice on the mountain of release.

We now come to the important period of the actual cataclysm—"The season which the sun god had fixed came round." This, as I shall show, seems to indicate that the festival occurred, or was supposed to occur, at the season of one of the solar festivals. And at that time the storm burst forth.

> " Then rose the water of dawn at daylight,
>   Like a dark cloud on the horizon of heaven ;
>   The Thunder god in the midst of it thundered—
>   Nebo and the Wind god march in front ;
>   The throne bearers go o'er mountain and plain ;
>   The Pestilence god brings with him affliction ;
>   The War god goes in front and casts down ;
>   The Angels of Earth carry the destruction ;
>   In their glory they sweep through the land ;
>   The deluge of the Rain god reaches to heaven ;
>   The darkened earth to waste is turned ;
>   The surface of the earth like fire they sweep—
>   They destroy all life from the face of the earth."

This poetic description of the terrible destruction that swept inland is a most graphic account of one of those terrible storms, such as that when the surveying ship Tigris was lost on the Euphrates, or such a storm as is described by Mr George Smith :—" On the 29th March, we fortunately got a change of horses. Soon after sunset the sky was covered with black clouds, so that it was difficult to find the tracks, and the thunderstorm came on. The thunder seemed as if it dashed itself against a range of mountains on our right, and then rolled back across the vast plain over which we were riding, while every now and then a vivid flash of lightning illuminated the whole scene, only to make the darkness more intense." We are not dependent upon modern travellers for

the descriptions of these terrible storms. Sennacherib in his Elamite war was stopped by the terrible
storms in the month Tebit. As he says—"The
advance I ordered in the month Tebit (December
and January), a terrible storm arose, and heaven and
earth it flooded. Rain upon rains, and snow the
channels filled." In like manner we find a record of
terrible storms in the month Sebat in the annals of
Esarhaddon (Budge, Hist. Esarhad., p. 23, line 14)—
"Snow storming in the month Sebat came; the
mighty darkness I feared not." I have quoted these
historical records of storms occurring during the
winter months as indicating the deluge season, and
the reason why the Deluge is assigned to the
eleventh tablet of the Gizdhubar legend, and equated
with the month Sebat—the month of the Curse of
Rain of the Akkadian calendar.

The rains of winter commence with the month
Dhebit or Thebit—a name meaning, as Dr F.
Delitzsch shows (Assy. and Heb., p. 16), the month
of "sinking in water." Its Akkadian name was Id-
Abba-Uddu, which may be rendered "the coming
forth of the Sea or Deluge;" while the next month
is, as we have seen, called Sebadh, or the month of
Destruction. This would seem to place the commencement of the Deluge at about the period of the
winter solstice. In support of this idea, too, we
find the Regent of the month Tebit is "Rimman, the
smiter of heaven and earth." The tablet of the

seasons, which I have already referred to, makes the season extending from 1st day of Kislen to the 30th day of Sebat—the period when the sun is in the orbit of Hea and the season of storms, using the same word as is used by Sennacherib and Esarhaddon. There is very little indication in the tablet as to the duration of the Deluge, but it seems to me to be based on a solar and climatological calculation. In order that we may understand that this description of the storm and deluge is not modern, on account of its poetic and graphic character, I quote the following from an ancient Akkadian hymn (W. A. I., IV., 19, 1) :—

1. The tempest from the midst of space has (gone forth),
2. The fate from the midst of heaven proceeds ;
3. It sweeps the earth like grass—
4. To the four winds its terror spreads like fire.
5. The men of the fields it causes affliction in their bodies ;
6. In the city and country it causes destruction to small and great ;
7. Strong one and servant bewail it.
8. In the heavens and earth like a waterspout it pours down ;
9. To the holy place of their god, they hasten and cry (aloud).

It is evident that both the Hebrew accounts and the Assyrian differ as to the duration of the Deluge ; yet all agree in its terrible character, and the universal destruction it brought with it. At the end of seven days, this wild and fearful tempest began to assuage. The Samas-Napisti opened the window of the ship, and wept, and was sad at heart at the ter-

rible destruction around him. We have next a
curious reference, which points to the astronomical
or solar character of the legend—"I looked at the
regions bounding the sea; to the twelve points there
was no land;" which clearly indicates, as I have
already stated, the knowledge of the Zodiac. We
now come to the resting of the ark—"To the country
of Nizir floated the ship; the mountain of Nizir
stopped (held) the ship, to pass over; it was not able
(col. iii. 32-3); and for seven days the ark remained
stranded." Now, where was this region of Nizir, and
what relation did it bear to the Biblical Ararat?
Upon this subject Professor Sayce has thrown much
important light in his paper on the " Cuneiform Inscriptions of Lake Van" (Journal R. A. S., vol. xiv.,
N.S., pt. 3). According to Biblical account, the ark
rested upon one of the mountains of Ararat, and " a
wide spread Eastern tradition" makes it Jebel Gudi.
This Gudi is the same as the Guti or Kuti of the inscriptions, and the " goim" or nations of the
Hebrews. The position of this district is accurately
fixed by the itineraries in the inscriptions of
Assurnazirpal (B.C. 886). This king states that, after
leaving Kalzu, near Arbela, he marched to the town
of Bairti and the land of Nizir. This fixes the district in the land of Pamir, a little south of Mt.
Rowandiz, the highest peak, and suggests that
Rowandiz was the spot where the Babylonian tradition made the ark rest. This mountain of Nizir is

the same as "the mountain of the East," the Olympus of the Akkadians. We know, from an astronomical tablet, that the east of the Akkadians was really the north-east. The east, we are told, is the land of Su-edina and Guti—that is, the mountains already referred to, and the lowland between them and the Tigris. We are also told that behind are Su-edina and Guti, thus pointing to this region of Kuti as the home from whence the people came, and the land they left behind them in their migration; thus it derived the name of "the mountain of the nations," and is evidently referred to by Isaiah (xiv. 13), where the king of Babylon is described as boasting that he "will ascend into heaven, and exalt his throne above the stars of the gods," and "will sit on the mountain of the assembly of the gods in the extremities of the north"—a position which points to this region near Rowandiz. It was therefore in this region that the Chaldeans placed the resting place of the ark. The tablet here again presents a difference from the Hebrew story, along with its agreement in general, as it also does with the versions of Berosus. The tablet says—"On the seventh day, in the course of it, I sent forth a dove; it went and turned; a resting place it saw not; it returned back. I sent forth a swallow; it left and turned; a resting place it could not see, and it returned back. I sent forth a raven, and it left. The raven went, and the corpses which were on the water it saw. It did eat,

it floated, and was carried away; it returned not"
Berosus states that the first time the birds were sent
forth they returned.   After an interval of some days,
he sent them forth a second time, and they returned
with their feet tinged with mud.   On the third trial
they returned no more.   In the tablet, we notice there
is no omen taken from the birds, as in Berosus, by
the mud on their feet; but the account of Berosus,
the tablet, and the Hebrew version are in agreement
in the birds being the raven and the dove, and in
the non-return of the former after being sent forth.
" He sent forth a raven, which went forth to and fro,
until the waters were dried up from off the earth"
(Gen. viii. 7).   The choice of the swallow is foreign
to both Berosus and the Hebrew writer.   The origin
of its selection is, however, shown in its Akkadian
name Sim-Khu, " the bird of fate "—omens, no doubt,
being derived from its flight.

We now come to the sacrifice of thanksgiving.   The altar, we are informed, is built on the
ziggurat, or peak of a mountain.   The use of this
word is peculiar and important.   We find the word
applied in the inscriptions to the lofty stage towers,
such as the great tower of E-Saggili, or that of
Khorsabad; and it was no doubt this ancient custom
of mountain sacrifices which led to the erection of
these lofty edifices on the plains of Chaldea.   The altar
was laid with reeds, pine, and spices; and now we
have a curious phrase—" The gods smelled the odour;

the gods smelled the sweet savour; the gods gathered
over the master of the sacrifice like flies;" which
accords so closely with the Hebrew version—"And
the Lord smelled the sweet savour" (Gen. vii. 21).
This sweet sacrifice to which the gods gathered like
flies was followed by the appearance of the rainbow
—"Then from afar the great goddess in her approach
raised up the zones which Anu had created as his
glory." The goddess here appears in a very similar
character to the Homeric Iris (Gladstone Primer
Homer, p. 81). The setting the bow in the clouds,
which is here identified as the bow of Anu, the god
of heaven, has its counterpart in the Hebrew version
—"And God said, I do set my bow in the clouds; it
shall be for a token of a covenant between me and
the earth" (Gen. ix. 13). The rainbow in the Chaldean Tablet does not appear in any way as a pledge
of a covenant between the gods and men; it is evidently here the bow of Istar, the daughter of Anu,
who bears the title of "archeress of the gods," and
who is often represented as carrying the sacred bow
of Anu, which found its representative in nature in
the rainbow. So far in our study of this tablet, we
have had a close agreement in the sequence of events
between the tablet and the Bible. The announce-
ment of the Deluge as a punishment for sin, the
order to build the ark or ship, the provisioning, the
embarkation of men and animals, the period of the
cataclysm, the stoppage on a mountain, the sacrifice

of thanksgiving, all follow in the same order in both accounts, though, as I have shown, varied in details.

We now come to marked differences. The first is in the establishment of the covenant with man that there should be no more deluges. I have already pointed out that it is to Bel, the lord of the earth, that the counsel to destroy all living things by a deluge is due; and so he is not present as the sacrifice of thanksgiving. But as he draws near to this high peak of the mountain of the gods, he sees the failure of his design in the ship resting on the peak —"His heart was filled with anger with gods and spirits. Let no man come forth alive; let no man escape the deep." In this idea of universal destruction, he has been defeated by the god who is the protector of Samas-Napisti, his family and city—"the god Hea, who knows all things;" and it is this god who acts as the mediator. Instead of a deluge, in future wild animals, lions, and jackals, or pestilence and famine, are to be the chastisers of mankind. Here we see that dread trinity of vengeance against which man has ever had to struggle—the warfare between men and the brute creation at first, followed by the warfare of men — famine and pestilence. So also in the Bible do we meet with this trinity, as—"I will consume them by the sword and by the famine and by the pestilence" (Jer. xiv. 12; xxvii. 13). So also is David given the choice of the famine, sword, or pestilence (2 Sam. xxiv. 15).

Both the lion and the jackal were emblems of the god of death. The jackal was called *Akhu*, "the evil (animal)." The Lik-Barra, or "evil dog" of the Akkadians, is the same as the word rendered "*Okhim*," "doleful creatures," in Isaiah xiii. 21, and was in ancient times, as at the present day, no doubt the inhabitant of grave-yards. There was found at Khorsabad a small statue of the god of death, represented with the head of a jackal.* The lion was the emblem of the god of war and of death—the "Ne-Uru-Gal," "the lord of the great city," "the city of the dead"—Sualu or Sheol. He was lord over the great city of Kuti or Kuthah (2 Kings xvii. 24-30), which was called by the Akkadians the city Tig-Abba, or "the city of the bowing down of the head," it being one of the great necropoli of Chaldea. The lions at the entrance to the royal palaces and temples were dedicated to him. After this mediation of Hea, the decision of the gods is revealed to the sage in a dream—"To Samas-Napisti a dream they sent, and the decision of the gods he heard" (col. iv. 22). Upon this decision never to destroy the earth again by a deluge, Bel, who had in the anger of his heart poured forth this destruction upon men, enters into the ship to meet Samas-Napisti and his wife—"He took my hand and raised me up ; he bade me rise, and united my wife to my side. He turned himself to us, and bound himself by a covenant to us, and blessed us" (col. iv. 24-26). The phrase *Izuiz*

* See next page.

THE GOD OF DEATH.

(Inzar), *ana bi-ri-in-ni* — "He was fixed to our bond"—may be compared with, "Behold, I will establish my covenant (beroth) with you" (Gen. ix. 11), where almost the same word is used; while the Divine blessing comes earlier in the chapter— "And God blessed Noah and his sons." After this we come to a very marked divergence from the Hebrew narrative in the translation of Samas-Napisti. Here there seems to have become woven into the Chaldean legend, which has hitherto so closely followed the Hebrew, an earlier incident—the translation of Enoch (Gen. v. 24). In the Bible the same epithet, "One who walked with God," is applied to both Noah and Enoch, and may resemble the words in the tablet—"I only was the servant of the great gods" (col. i. 13). In the accounts given by Berosus, we have a similar story of the translation; but in that of Eusebius, the gods seem to have removed the sage to heaven, as we read — "Him they saw no more, but they could distinguish his voice in the air;" but in that of Abydenus, it is simply stated that "the gods translated him from among men." Here the legend of the Deluge ends, the remainder of the tablet being occupied by the account of the cure of the disease of Gizdhubar, and his return to Uruk or Erech, his capital city.

With regard to the names of the translated sage (Samas-Napisti, Xisuthrus, and Noah) in the three

accounts under consideration, something may be said.
The first of these means "the Sun of Life," or the
"Living Sun," and the reason of its adoption seems
to me to be a climatological one. From the time of
the autumnal equinox until past the winter solstice,
the sun is weak and powerless in the regions of
winter. Thus as in Phœnicia we have the legend of
the dead Tammuz, so in the weak and dying solar
hero Gizdhubar we have a similar idea embodied.
The sun is not dead, but comes forth again and begins
gradually to assert its power in the month Nisan of
the Semites, the month of "the beginning or coming
forth" (Del., Ass., and Hebr., p. 15). This month
was called by the Akkadians 10. Par-Ziggar, the
month of the "altar of the mountain ;" and we know
the word "Ziggurat," a mountain peak, is used to
express the position of the altar built on coming out
of the ark (Col. iii. 46). This group is also explained
as "the dwellers at the holy altar" (W. A. I. ii., 35-
55). These facts seem to point to the altar from
which the month derived its name being connected
with the altar built by Samas-Napisti. If this is the
case, then we may regard the name Samas-Napisti as
the Sun-god preserved through the deluge of winter,
and coming forth in the spring time like Noah from
the ark. The tablet of divine regents of the months
make Anu and Bel the rulers of this month, and we
have seen what a prominent part the latter takes in
the sacrifice and covenant. In the tablet a very

important epithet is applied to Samas-Napisti—he is always called .Rūku, "the remote" or far distant, implying his translation. With regard to the name Xisuthrus, it appears to me, as I have already suggested, to be a Greek form of the ancient name of Anu Zi-Susru, "Spirit of the Founder," and belongs to the time when Anu absorbed so many of the epithets of the other gods, as is shown by the tablet in which all the chief persons in the Creation legends are regarded as manifestations of the great father of the gods.

The age of the legend is difficult to ascertain, but of its antiquity there can be no doubt. The close resemblance of many of the passages to the Akkadian hymns, and the fact that in some copies the scribe, who has made his version from older copies, has inserted the archaic characters where he has not known their modern equivalents, would carry the tablet certainly back to the third millenium before our era. Like all legends, it shows evidence of growth from a simpler original—the narrative in some places being confused by the improper blending of the versions. It differs from the Hebrew account in its polytheism, but that polytheism is not so strongly asserted as first appears—the high, almost supreme, position given to Hea, as I have remarked, causing it to differ from many other Babylonian legends. In regard to its age I can say nothing definite, but I feel certain that the account, perhaps

E

in a slightly different form, was current in Chaldea as early as b.c. 2120—about the time when Abraham left Chaldea. In this lecture I have not entered upon any criticism of the Hebrew narrative; that work I leave to others far more competent than myself; my chief object has been to place before those who wish to employ these records of the past the means of applying them to Biblical criticism.

CHALDEAN LIBRARIES.

BEROSUS, the Chaldean historian, resorts to an ingenious literary fiction to preserve the continuity of narrative in his "History of Chaldea," which he claims to have based on documentary evidence, extending back over a period of twenty myriads of years. The deluge, which forms the concluding episode in the first book, and his account of which is, as I have shown, based upon the copies of the story of Samas-Napisti stored in the libraries of Chaldea, causes no rupture in the long series of records to which he claims to have had access; for by the ingenious device of making Xisuthrus an author and historian, he is able to carry his series of records beyond the dividing streams of the deluge. Xisuthrus was, according to Berosus, instructed by the god Cronos, whom we can identify with Hea of the tablet, before the deluge, to write a history of "the beginning, progress, and end of all things up to that time, and to deposit these records in Sippar of the Sun, where in after time they would be found by the survivors, and form the first chapters of Chaldean history." But even this primitive sire of the Chaldeans, the pious Xisuthrus, cannot lay claim to be the founder of Babylonian literature; for the earliest chapters of his historical work were transmitted to him by a still more remote author, Annedotos-Oannes, called Musaros, to whom Berosus attributes the writings of the Chaldean Book of Origins. In claiming for the national literature so vast an age, and carrying its records back thus far into the azure of the past, Berosus affords us a strong proof of his being a member of the scribe caste. To these ancient Chaldean *gens de lettres* their profession was all things; its history was the history of the world ; in the time when there was no literature there was no world. They could find no better description of chaos than the time when "in those days no record was written." Berosus, in carrying back his authorities to so remote a period, is but acting up to the traditions of his order, who saw in the Musaros-Oannes, who rose from the sea to teach men the rudiments of civilisation, arts, and letters, the founder of their caste.

The account which Berosus gives of this mysterious founder of the scribe caste is :—" In the beginning there were in Babylon a great number of men of various races, who had colonised Chaldea. They lived without laws, after the manner of animals.

But in the first year there appeared coming out of the Erythrian Sea (Persian Gulf), on the coast where it borders Babylonia, an animal endowed with reason, named Oannes. He had all the body of a fish, but below the head of the fish another head, which was that of a man, also the feet of a man, which came out of its fish's tail. He had a human voice, and its image is preserved to this day. This animal passed the day time among men, taking no nourishment. It taught them use of letters, of sciences, and of arts of every kind, the rules for the foundation of towns and the building of temples, the principles of laws and geometry, the sowing of seeds and the harvest; in one word, it gave to men all that conduced to the enjoyment of life. Since that time nothing excellent has been invented. At the time of sunset this monster Oannes threw itself into the sea, and passed the night beneath the waves, for it was amphibious. He wrote a book upon the beginning of all things, and of civilisation, which he left to mankind." (Berosus Frag. i., Edit. Lenormant.) Helladice quotes the same story, and calls the composite being Oes; while another writer, Hyginus, calls him Euahanes. It is evident, M. Lenormant remarks, that this latter name is more correct than Oannes, for it points to one of the Akkadian names of Hea Hea—Khan, "Hea the fish,"—and must be identified with the fish-headed god so often represented on the sculptures from Nimroud (B. M , N. G ,

No. 29), and clay figures have been found at Nimroud and Khorsabad, as well as numerous representations on seals and gems. We have already seen how Hea has the titles of " he who knows all things," "the god of wisdom," and his abode was in the Absie or mysterious deep, the house of wisdom. It was therefore to Hea, the Oannes of Berosus, that the Babylonian scribes traced their origin. The god Hea had other descendants beside his mediatorial son Merodach, the chief being—

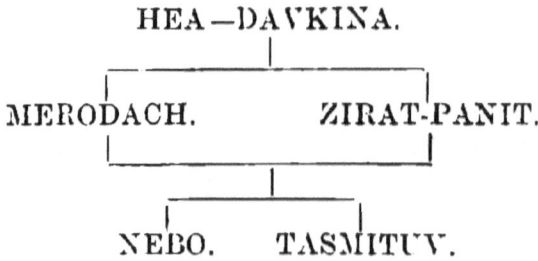

The titles which Nebo assumes are those which show that he had taken very much the place of his grandfather Hea as the god of learning. In a tablet which gives his numerous titles (W. A. I. ii., 60, No. 2), we find him called " the son of Merodach," "the first-born lord," "the binder of all," "the maker of oracles," "the maker of writings on written tablets," "the wise god," "the lord of illustrious knowledge," " the clearer-up of difficulties," "the enlarger of the ears or mind," "the maker of inscriptions." All these titles mark him as the Hermes of Chaldea.

His name, Nabū, means the Prophet, and he is associated with a goddess, Tasmituv, "the Hearer," a relationship which reminds us very much of that of master and pupil.

There is a bilingual hymn to this god in Akkadian and Assyrian, which brings before us the position of the divinity in Chaldea (W. A. I. iv., 20, No. 3):—

Oh Lord, by thy wisdom, a wisdom unequalled.
Nebo, by thy wisdom, a wisdom unequalled.
By thy temple of E-Zida, a temple unequalled.
By thy city of Borsippa, a city unequalled.
By thy field of Babylonia, a field unequalled.
By thy weapon . . . which from its mouth death pours not
    forth.
Blood is not shed.
Thy command, as heaven is unchangeable, in heaven thou
    art supreme.

The temple of E-Zida, the house of knowledge, was the shrine of this great god in the city of Borsippa, the site of which is now marked by the ruins of the Birs Nimrūd. This was the great centre of Babylonian learning, the *alma mater* of the scribe caste.

I now pass to what may be called the historical evidence of the remote antiquity of the scribe caste. Turning to our oldest inscription of which the date is fixed by indisputable facts, we are met at once with evidence of the great antiquity of writing and writers in Chaldea. The inscriptions of Sargon of Agadhe or Akkad, and Naram Sin, are now known by the twice repeated statement in two cylinders of Nabonidus to date from B.C. 3750. These two inscriptions read thus—

No. I.	No. II.
1. Sar-Ga-Ni.	1. Na-Ra-Am Dp. En-Zu (Sin).
2. Sar Lukh.	2. Sar.
3. A-Ga-De.	3. Ki-Ib-Ra-Tim.
4. A-na.	4. Ar-Ba-Im.
5. Il Samas Ki (Sipar).	5. Sar.
6. In. Ud Kip-nun-ki.	6. A-pi-Ra-Ak.
7. A-mu-ra.	7. Ma-Gan (Ki).

The first of these inscriptions reads — " Sargon, the good king of Agadhe (Akkad) ; to the Sun god, within Sippara, I looked."

The second—" Naram Sin, king of the four quarters ; the lands of Apirak and Magan."

Both these documents are written, not in the most ancient language of Chaldea, but in a language which will at once be recognised as good Semetic, akin to Hebrew. The words *Arbaim*, " four ; " *Sar*, " king ; " *Naram*, " beloved ; " *Kiprat*, " border ; " *Amuru*, " I looked," all find their analogy in the Hebrew lexicon.

But we must remember that it is more universally admitted by all Assyrian scholars that the cuneiform mode of writing with its compiled syllabary, with ideographs, polyphones, &c., and its texts reading from left to right, could not be the invention of a Semetic people. M. Renan, a master of Semetic paleography and learning, who at one time could not understand this abnormal character of the Assyrian inscriptions, now writes :—" No one in the present day can doubt that this Turanian civilisation possessed, and most probably created, the writing called cuneiform." Yet here, at the remote period of thirty-eight centuries before the Christian era, we are brought face to face with a remarkable problem. This writing, once pictorial, as both Mr Houghton and myself have shown, has passed through the ideographic into the phonetic stage, and become borrowed and adapted to the requirements of a language of a totally different family and genus. Indeed, Berosus, considering how slowly these changes took place when there was but little civilising friction, had more grounds for his statement than we imagined. With all this retrospective enlargement of the use of writing, we get a similar expansion of the tradition and history of these scribe castes, and even at this time we find them in existence and in power. In the collection of M. le Clerc of Paris is a seal, which bears the inscription—" Sar-Ga-Ni, Sar Lukh, Agadhe, Ibni-Sarru, Dip-Sar Ardusu ?"—" To

Sargon, the good ? king of Akkad, Ibni-Sarru, the scribe, his servant." This inscription, written in very archaic characters, is the oldest charter we at present have of the antiquity of the scribes of Chaldea. Another seal, which belongs to a little later date than this, is to be seen in the British Museum, and bears on it the inscription of " Debu, the recorder of the king . . . the scribe, his servant." (Figured in Tomkin's Life of Abraham, pl. 3). In the sister Empire of Egypt, the scribes were a caste of great antiquity, and holding high rank in the community; and the description by Dr Brugsch of this class may assist us in an arrangement of the scribes of Babylonia. " Of a more peaceful charac- ter," he says, " was the much-praised office of *Hir Shesta*," which means " teacher of the secret," for they possessed all the hidden wisdom of those times. Those learned in the secrets of the heavens looked upwards, and explained the ever-changing courses of the stars. This class find their counterpart in the numerous Lu-Aba, or " men of the month ;" the " astronomers " of Chaldea, as Professor Sayce sug- gests, while the former class are represented by the officials who bear the titles of " He who opens the eyes," the instructor (W. A. I., v. 13, 13), and others also who are called " Abgallu," counsellors, wise men, and perhaps the lawyer is represented by the official called *Bel teriti*, " lord of laws," mentioned in the same tablet. The ordinary scribes bore the titles or name of "*Sapri*," scribes, or Dip-Sar, "the tablet writer." There were other officials of this class—the librarian, who had charge of the tablets; and the man who had charge of the papyri. There were scribes attached to each law court and temple, and many hundreds of their names are found attached to the legal, commercial, and fiscal documents. We may conclude, therefore, that the scribe caste was a large and an ancient one in Chaldea. I may notice that there must have been attached to the Assyrian Court during the time of the Sargonides a body of scribes, who had attained a very high skill in caligraphy. The writing of some of the tablets and cylinders is so minute and so perfect as to be nearly equal to fine engraver's work. I may quote, as examples of this work, the fragments of a cylinder of Sargon II. (B.C. 721), recording the expedition against Ashdod; in the *Daily Telegraph* collection, also two tablets of a mythological character (K.G. case B), which are even finer and more minute work. It was this caste of brothers of the style who year by year, century by century, went labouring on, building up that grand temple of culture, the learning and wisdom of Chaldea, that glorious product of the combined mental efforts of the plodding, inventive Akkadian mind, and the receptive, poetic, and progressive mind of the Semite, which has done more for Western learning than we can estimate. All this learning has for more than 6000 years lain buried beneath the desert sands ; now opens it the treasure houses of its hidden secrets to the eyes of astonished posterity. There is an ancient Arab saying which seems to place vividly before us one lesson of this resurrection of the writings of the past. It says :— " There is no writer that shall not perish, but what his hand has written shall endure. Write nothing therefore but what will please thee when thou shalt see it on day of resurrection." Little did the Chaldean scribe, who long years ago wrote on the plastic clay the glory of his king or the scandal of the bazaar, think that tens of centuries after, in a far-distant isle of the setting sun, his words would be read with eager interest by his fellow-men.

With so powerful a caste of scribes, there must naturally have been a large number of libraries. Indeed, every temple had its library, but of the chief libraries a few only are known to us. The chief library of all Babylonia was that of the temple of Nebo at Borsippa. It was from this library that Assurbanipal took many of the inscriptions which he placed in his new public library at Nineveh, and the Ninivite library was named after its Babylonian prototype. There was also a library in the temple at Sippara dedicated to the Sun god. There must have been a library containing a number of astronomical tablets here, as the library of Sargon of Agadhe or Akkad was placed here ; and it was to him the great work on astronomy in seventy tablet books was attributed.

In Kute or Kutha, the site of which is marked by the mound of Tel Ibrahim, was a library, and, judging from the Cutha Creation Tablet, it seems to have been a very ancient one, and taught somewhat differently on religious matters from other libraries. Ur and Erech had libraries, and at Larsa, the modern Senkereh, the Ellassar of Gen. xiv. 1, there were mathematicians, some of whose works are preserved to us. In the examination of so vast a library of learning as these tablets form, embracing every section of literature, it is difficult to know where to commence. As, however, these mathematical and geographical tablets are among the oldest tablets of the series, I will briefly describe them. The most important are two lists of square and cube roots and a tablet of measures. These important documents were found at Larsa. The text is published in W. A. I., vol. iv., pl. 40. The table of square roots gives the roots and squares from 1-60, and that of cubes from 1-32. The scale adopted is that of units of 1-10, 60-600, 3600—the 60 being called the *susu* or sos; 600 the *neru* or naros; and 3600 the *sar* or sarros; and, with this sexigesimal scale, most complicated problems could be worked. For example, to express the square of 50, the scribe wrote what at first looked like 1.41.40, really representing $60 \times 41 + 40 = 2500$; and in the higher numbers, as, for example, the cube of 32 = 9.6.8 = $9 \times 60^2 + 6 \times 60 + 8 = 32,768$, the cube of 32.

SQUARE ROOTS.

$$1.40 \ (\ 1 \times 60 + \ 4) = \quad 64, \text{ the square of } 8.$$
$$2. \ 1 \ (\ 2 \times 60 + \ 1) = 121, \quad ,, \quad\quad ,, \quad 11.$$
$$3.45 \ (\ 3 \times 60 + 45) = 225, \quad ,, \quad\quad ,, \quad 15.$$
$$56. \ 4 \ (56 \times 60 + \ 4) = 3364, \quad ,, \quad\quad ,, \quad 58.$$
$$58. \ 1 \ (58 \times 60 + \ 1) = 3481, \quad ,, \quad\quad ,, \quad 59.$$
$$1.... \ (60 \times 60) \quad\quad = 3600, \quad ,, \quad\quad ,, \quad 60.$$

CUBE TABLE.

$$1. \ 4 \ (1 \times 60 + \ 4) = \ 64, \text{ the cube of } 4.$$
$$2. \ 5 \ (2 \times 60 + \ 5) = 125, \quad ,, \quad\quad ,, \quad 5.$$
$$3.36 \ (3 \times 60 + 36) = 216, \quad ,, \quad\quad ,, \quad 6.$$

With the longer figures the third element of the scale comes in—

$$1. \ 8.16 \ (1 \times 3600 + \ 8 \times 60 + 16) = 4096 = \text{the cube of } 16$$
$$1.21.53 \ (1 \times 3600 + 21 \times 60 + 53) = 4913 = \quad ,, \quad 17$$
$$8.16.31 \ (8 \times 3600 + 16 \times 60 + 31) = 29791 = \quad ,, \quad 31$$
$$9. \ 6. \ 8 \ (9 \times 3600 + \ 6 \times 60 + \ 8) = 32768 = \quad ,, \quad 32$$

This system may seem a little strange and cumbrous to us at first sight, but it is surprising how exactly it coincides with our every day numeration. Thus we write 61, which really stands for $6 \times 10 + 1 = 61$; or we write the cube of 31 as 29791, which is really $29 \times 10^3 + 7 \times 10^2 + 9 \times 10^1 + 1$, as the Babylonian is $8 \times 60^2 + 16 \times 60^1 + 31$. In like manner we learn that in their expression of fractions they employed their scale of 60 as we employ ours of 10 in decimals. Thus we write $1.5 = 1\frac{1}{2} = 1\frac{5}{10}$, they wrote $1^{30} = 1\frac{30}{60} = 1\frac{1}{2}$. So $1\frac{1}{3} = 1^{20}$ or $1\frac{20}{60}$, $1\frac{1}{3} = 1^{10}$, $1\frac{1}{4} = 1^{15} = 1\frac{15}{60}$, the unit of 60 being the understood denominator as we use 10 in decimals. This same scale furnished their divisions of the measures of length, as in the table of measures given by the late Dr Lepius of Berlin, in his work, entitled, " Die Babylonische-Assyrischen Längenmasse, Berlin, 1877, from which I have derived most of this information. Here we find—

5 Uban (fingers)	= 1 Kat (Hand).
6 Kat	= 1 Ammat or cubit.
6 Ammat	= 1 Kan (Reed).
120 Kan	= 1 Susu.
30 Susu	= 1 Kaspu.

In like manner we find the great circle of the heavens, the yearly round of the sun, divided into 60×6, or 360 days. That they applied their mathematical skill to mensuration and surveying is shown in the carefully-drawn plan from Tel Lo, already referred to (Lect. I.), and a still more elaborate example is now in the British Museum, which represents the survey of a Babylonian estate, in which every dimension of each plot of land is figured as carefully as a modern survey, and the names of adjacent properties or boundaries given.*

Chaldea has always been regarded as the birthplace

* See next page.

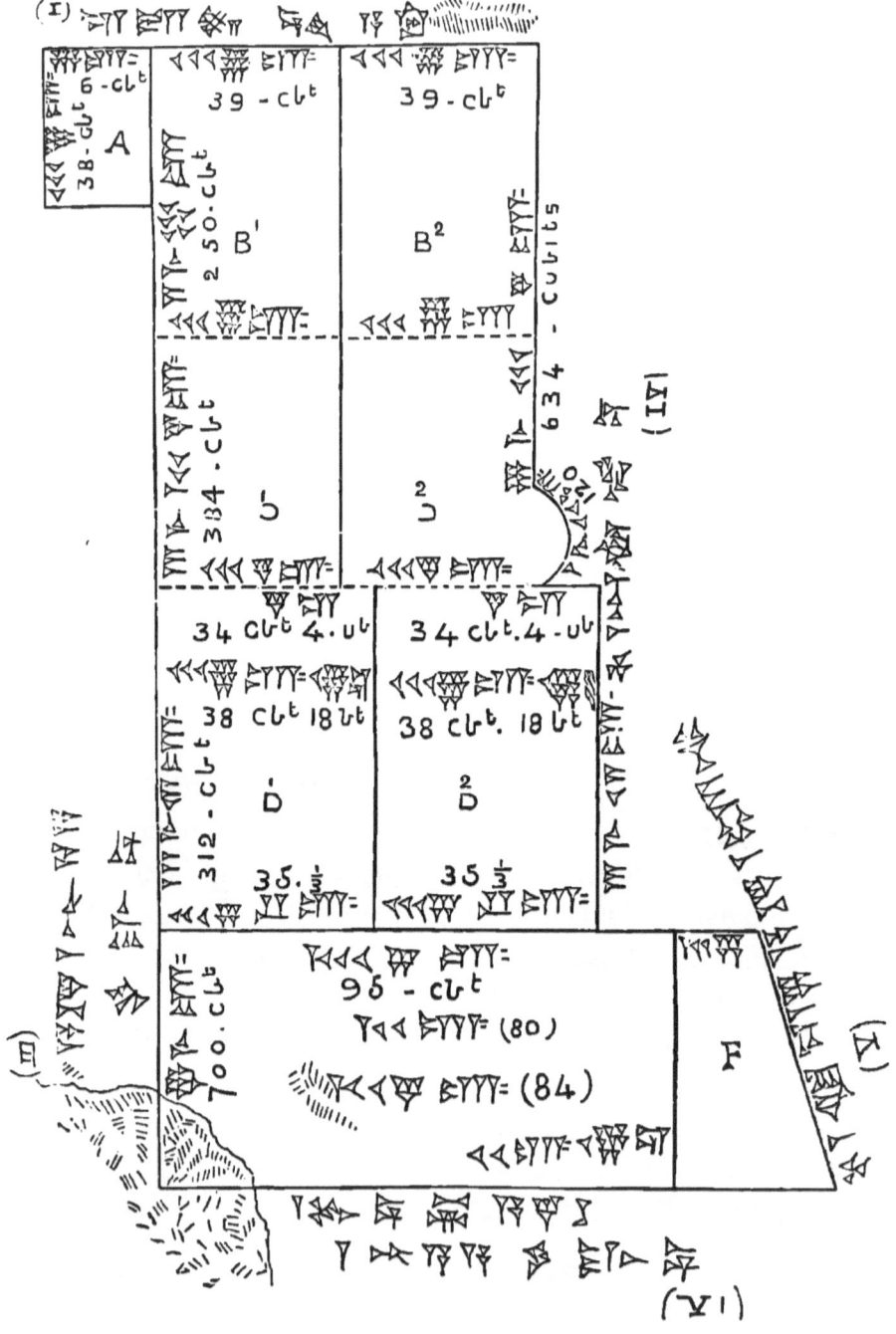

of astronomy, so much so, that the word Chaldean has become almost a synonym for an astronomer or astrologer. Some of the writers among the classics ascribe a fabulous antiquity to Chaldean astronomy. According to Epigenes, these observations had been carried back 720,000 years. Berosus says 470,000. The Babylonians themselves attributed the codification of all astronomical knowledge, and its embodiment in a work, entitled Namar Beli, "The Illumination of Bel" to Sargon of Akkad, whose reign we see has to be placed at B C. 3750 to 3800. There is a long inscription, an Assyrian copy of a Babylonian tablet, of this king's reign, describing his campaigns in Syria, Elam, &c., and each expedition is preceded by the omen which foretold its results. I quote a few extracts from it (W. A. I. iv., 34, 1):—"At the time when the moon in its whole mass and the under part is full, and above a clear sky, and behind makes it large and bright. Sargon, according to this omen, to the land of Martu (Syria) marched, the land of Martu he swept, and the four quarters his hand captured."

"When the moon is like a cloud, and the orb a horn has not, on the right of the orb opposition is made, and on the left against it the seven confront." Sargon upon this omen — The inhabitants of his land, all of it, revolted against him, and in Akkad enclosed him. Sargon came forth, their bodies he smote, and their destruction he accomplished." These divinations, by the way, and such consulting of the

omens Ezekiel (xxi. 21, 22) refers to in the words—
" For the king of Babylon standeth at the parting
of the way, at the head of two ways; he hath
made bright (or shaken) his arrows, he consulted the
images (teraphim), he looked in the liver," were
common occurrences before and during campaigns.
Of this we have historical evidence of great interest.
In about the year 1130 B.C., a prince named Nebuchadnezzar seized the throne of Babylon after a
period of anarchy. During his reign a comet
appeared, which is thus described by a Babylonian
astronomer (W. A. I. iii., 52, 1):—

1. The star rose, its rays were bright as the day.
2. With its rays like a creeping thing, a scorpion, a tail it
   forms.
3. The observation of the eyes was favourable,
4. Pleasing the lord of this house, and all the land.
5. At that time when even a lord there was not in all the
   land,
6. Rebellion, sin, defection there was. A strong one is
   exalted
7. ——— the master of that house, and that king
8. By right is established. Obedience and peace in the
   land are.
9. These things from the (Star),
10. The great star from the northern orbit
11. To the southern orbit.
12. In its extent like a creeping thing, a scorpion, a tail.
13. It makes turning (upwards) ———
14. In its position, in the abode ———
15. Of Bel it fills.

16. This is, according to the tablet,
17. When Nebuchadnezzar, the king, on the land of Elam seized.

As this tablet comes from the royal library at Nineveh, and was transcribed by order of Assur-banipal, who reigned B.C. 664, it cannot be the Nebuchadnezzar the Great. Of this Elamite campaign we have historical record upon the stone memorial of this expedition, which is now exhibited in the Nimroud gallery of the British Museum. On it Scorpion-saggitarius representing this comet is carved. Later still we meet with a curious example of the influence of astrology on the kings of Assyria. In the year B.C. 673, when Esarhaddon was starting on his Egyptian campaign, the following event is recorded in a tablet of the astronomical library (K. 2701):—

1. The god Assur, in a dream, to the father of the king my lord, the just prince. . . . .
2. The king, the lord of kings, the heart of hearts (grandson) of the just prince. . . . .
3. Thou shalt restore the wisdom of the house of wisdom (Absic). and all the people. . . . .
4. When the father of the king my lord to the land of Egypt went,
5. Into the grooves of Kharran, the dwelling of the god of the cedar tree, he went.
6. The moon over the corn fields stood, having two crowns on his head (with a double halo round it),
7. While Nusku (Evening Star) stood at his side. The father of the king my lord entered, and

8. The crown on his (Assurbanipal's) head he placed, and the government of the countries he gave him.
9. And when the road Egypt he took, the blessing of the countries followed him.

It is evident that this accidental aspect of the moon was construed by the court party into the means of forcing the king to settle the government of the country before leaving on a perilous expedition into Egypt. The opening lines of this tablet are very remarkable, as they seem to throw light upon the king's great work of founding a public library at Nineveh for the instruction of the people: "Thou shalt restore the wisdom of the house of wisdom, and all the people. . . ." It is unfortunate that the last few lines are lost. In the colophon attached to the tablets in the royal library we read that the king invokes Nebo and Tasmituv, who have opened his eyes and enlarged his ears (mind) to all the wisdom of the tablets which he has had copied and explained, that is translated, and placed in his palace for the instruction of his people. This library, a large portion of the contents of which are now in the British Museum, was one of the most remarkable institutions in the world. Founded, as we know, from a purely political motive, it preserved to us learning, and wisdom, and records of remote history which might have been for ever lost had it not been for the enterprise of Assurbanipal. The loss of the Alexandrian library is often bemoaned by Western scholars, but here in the terra cotta tablets of the library of Assurbanipal we have the *editio prima* of many of the choicest treasures of the Egyptian library. Every branch of literature finds a place on its shelves, and it is arranged in a manner so systematic and complete that it might well form an example to the curators of many a European library. Consisting of at least 100,000 tablet-books, we can see from the numbering and sectional arrangement there would be far less difficulty for the student to obtain his terra cotta tome in the Bibliotheque Nationale d'Assyrie than in many a modern public library.

THE LEGENDS OF GIZDHUBAR.

THE EPIC OF CHALDEA.

THE discovery and decipherment of the Chaldean Deluge Legend, some twelve years ago, opened up an entirely new section of Assyrian literature. The patient researches of the small band of Assyriologists had gathered fragment by fragment, like the tesseræ of some shattered mosaic, from the oblivion which for centuries had shrouded it, and from inscriptions, which for centuries had been silent, the story of Assyria's kings. They had given to the world's history a retrospective enlargement, far beyond the expectations of the most ardent student of antiquity. Although the annals of the life and times, and the record of those deeds of war and conquest, which had emblassoned the names of Sargon, Sennacherib, and Assurbanipal, the Sardanapalus of the Greeks, on the roll of history, had now been restored to the student, there was a large section of the cuneiform literature untouched. The great library of Nineveh, which had been rescued from beneath the dust of ages by Sir Henry Layard and his able lieutenant, Mr Hormuzd Rassam, was not merely a chamber of royal records. Its contents had a far larger range, embracing, as we now know, almost every branch of literature. During the twelve years which have elapsed since Mr George Smith startled the world by his discovery, the treasure-house which he opened has been very zealously searched by ardent students, and the result has been the revealing to a learning and wisdom, equalled, but not surpassed, by any nation of antiquity, except perhaps the Celestial Empire, to whose literature, in many respects, it affords a striking resemblance.

I now pass to the system and arrangement of this ancient and long-buried library, which has yielded us such valuable records of the long bygone past. The key to the arrangement, and the extensive and varied character of the library, is afforded by the colophon attached to each tablet, which resembles in some respect our dedication and title-pages. The most frequent one reads as follows :—" The palace of Assur-bani-abla, king of nations, king of Assyria, of whom Nebo and Tasmituv have enlarged his ears and enlightened his eyes to the wealth of the tablets, of which the kings going before him (his ancestors), their writing had not reverenced. The wisdom of Nebo. . . . All there was on the tablets I wrote,

I studied, I explained, and, for the instruction of my people, within my palace I placed." The existence of a series of instruction tablets, such as the syllabaries, and the important series of bilingual tablets in parallel columns, classified as the series *Ana itti su,* "to be with him," literally "handbooks," indicate the educational character of the library. In the same manner the statement *ki pi duppi u tamadi labruti makhruti Assuriu Akkadi*—"According to the tablets and ancient teaching side by side of Assur and Akkad;" and sometimes we find—"According to the ancient tablets and papyri side by side of Assur, Sumir, and Akkad" (W. A. I., III., 52, 2). In the case of the former, it evidently applies to the bilingual tablets, in which the languages of Assyrian and Akkad, or North Babylonia, are placed side by side ; and, in the latter, to the trilingual tablets, in which the versions of the languages of Assyria, Akkad, and Sumir, the Shinar of the Hebrews, or South Babylonia, are placed together, as in the lexographical tablet printed in W. A. I., vol. IV., pl. 11-12. These statements, together with the often-repeated phrase, *Kima labri su,* like its old copy, attached to the majority of tablets—the Gizdhubar legends included —show, as we know from history, that the library of Assurbanipal was the product of a royal library commission appointed about B.C. 660 to copy all the most important tablets in the libraries of Chaldea, and to place them in the library at Nineveh—the objec being to stay the intercourse between the Babylonian priests and the youths of Assyria, which had caused so much trouble during the rebellions of Merodach, Baladan, and Samas-suma-ukin.

It has been necessary for me thus to preface my paper with this outline of the origin and system of the royal library at Nineveh, in order that we may better ascertain the position of the Gizdhubar poem in the literature of Assyria. I will now pass to the subject of classification of the tablet books adopted by the Assyrian scribes. The system resembled in some respects that adopted by the Hebrew scribes in the naming the books by their first words, as Genesis, Exodus, and Leviticus are called respectively בְּרֵאשִׁית (Bereshith), שְׁמוֹת (Shemoth), and וַיִּקְרָא (Wayyikra)—these being the opening words of each. In like manner, we find the Assyrian and Babylonian scribes cataloguing the majority of their tablet books according to the first words of their first tablet. Thus the first creation tablet commences with the words Enuva Elis—"In the time when as yet on high." So we find the Fifth Tablet, which contains an account of the creation of the heavenly bodies, classified as "Tablet V."—Enuva Elis. That is, the Fifth Tablet of the series commencing with those words. The magical tablets are catalogued under the heading Atal limnuti—"evil spirits"—being the opening words of the First Tablet. The Penitential Psalms under the words Salmu arka—"future peace"

At the end of the Deluge Tablet is the following colophon or docket :—

I. First Line of Next Tablet of the Series.

The Tambūkku in the house of the   was left.

II. Number of Tablet in Series.

Eleventh Tablet (of series)—"He who the fountain had seen. The story of Gizdhubar.

III. Statement of Copying from Older Documents.

Like its old copy, written and made clear.

The general title of the series may from this be taken to be Zikar Gizdhubar, "the story of Gizdhubar"—*zikar* being the construct case of *zikaru*, a record or memorial from *zakaru* to record the Hebrew דָכַר, "to remember, to bring to mind." There are portions of two other sets of these stories—one fairly complete, the other only mentioned by name. The first of these is called *Zikar Dibbara*—"the story of the Pestilence god," and relates to a terrible plague sent as divine punishment on the land of Babylonia by the offended gods. Of the story we have fragments of those tablets out of a series of seven. In the fable of the ox and the horse, mention is made of the "story of Istar, a legend," as yet lost to us, though, as I shall show, referred to in the Sixth Tablet of the Gizdhubar story. Sir Henry Rawlinson was, I believe, the first to point out the solar character of the Epic, and to show that its twelve

books were arranged according to the sun's journey
through the twelve signs of the zodiac. More fragments of the Epic itself, and tablets relating to it,
having been brought to light, his conjecture has been
amply confirmed. It has long been known that the
majority of the signs of the zodiac are represented by
the names of the Akkadian months, and that even
where the names themselves do not agree, there is
other evidence forthcoming, such as the character of
the divine regent of the month, or the name of the
ruling star, which agrees with the zodiacal sign.
The following general statements as to the arranging
of the twelve constellations may be quoted as
examples. In the Fifth Creation Tablet (lines 1-
7) :—

1. He made pleasant the dwelling-places of the great gods.
2. The constellations, their forms as animals he fixed.
3. The year its divisions he divided.
4. Twelve months of constellations by threes he fixed.
5. From the day by which the year commences to its end.
6. He determined the position of the crossing stars, and
   fixed their bounds.
7. Not to make fault or error of any kind.

Also in an astronomical tablet (W. A. I., vol. III.,
pl.), we read—"Twelve months to each year, 360
days (60 × 6) in number as recorded." And again in
the Deluge Tablet (Col. iii. 30-31)—"I looked to the
regions bounding the sea. To the twelve points no
land I saw." In addition to these very distinct
allusions to the division of the great circle into

twelve parts, we have the fact that nearly all the emblems of the constellations of the zodiac are found on the monuments, especially the seals and boundary stones. The text of all known fragments of the Epic have been published in *fac-simile* in Delitzsch-Assyriologisch-Bibliothzk by Dr Paul Haupt of Leipzic; and he has, I believe, written a discurtative upon the Epic, but this I have not had the advantage of seeing.

In the accompanying table, I have arranged the months with the signs of the zodiac, the divine regents, and the name given to Merodach, the star of Babylon—the morning star referred to in Isaiah xiv. 12. I think it will be at once seen how much evidence there is of zodaical arrangement both of the calendar and the books of the Epic.

It will be observed that I differ somewhat in my arrangement of the tablets from Mr Smith, but it must be remembered that we have only the number dockets attached to Tablets III., VI., X., XI., XII.— all other fragments having to be arranged according to incident. The numbered tablets, however, all fall well into their places under signs corresponding to their stories. An examination of the text of the tablets that the Epic is a collection of national stories woven together, and all centred round " Gizdhubar, the perfect in strength "—Dp. Gizdhubar. Gitmalu.[1]

Not *Buralu*, as read by Mr Smith, but a derivative from *gamalu*—" perfect."

Emuki. The Achilles of this Chaldean Iliad, who was ruler of Uruki, the Erech of Genesis (x. 10). This city throughout the legends is called Uruk-Su Buri—"Erech, the beautiful or blessed"—a phrase which calls very forcibly to mind the "golden troy" of Homer. The fact that some of the stories are woven together by a very slender thread is quite apparent when the text comes to be examined, and there is no more glaring example than that of the Deluge Tablet, which is clearly interpolated whole-sale into the text of Tablet XI., and its commence-ment timed off. This was done in order to obtain a legend corresponding to the sign of Aquarius, and to the month of the "curse of rain" of the Akkadians, the month Sebadhu, or "destruction" of the Semites. Again, in the Sixth Tablet, we have a number of small stories of the loves of Istar, evidently older than the Epic, woven into the speech of Gizdhubar. Of the First Tablet we have no trace, nor do we gain any indication of its contents. The fragment Mr Smith placed as the commencement of the Epic, if it belongs at all to the poem, certainly does not come in this place. Of the second book, we have some fragments; and from the continuation of the story in the third, we are able to gather a fair knowledge of the nature of its contents. As corresponding to the sign of Taurus, and the month of the Protecting Bull, it relates to the mysterious satyr or centaur, the companion of the hero so often represented on

the Babylonian cylinder seals. Gizdhubar has a
dream that the stars of heaven are falling upon him,
and, like Nebuchadnezzar, we can find no one to
explain the hidden meaning to him. He is, however, told by his huntsman, Zaidu, of a very wise
creature who dwells in the marshes, three days'
journey from Erech. The introduction of this personage, Za-Ai-Du—"the hunter" (Heb. צוּד and
צוּד) into the story, brings before us very forcibly the
גִּבֹּר צִיד—"mighty hunter"—of Genesis x. 9. The
strange being whom this companion of the hero is
despatched to bring to the court is one of the most
interesting characters in the Epic. He is called
Hea-Bani—"he whom Hea has made." This mysterious creature is represented on the gems as half a
man and half a bull. He has the body, face, and
arms of a man, and the horns, legs, hoofs, and tail of
a bull. Though in form rather resembling the
satyrs, and in fondness for and association with the
cattle the rustic deity Pan, yet in his companionship
with Gizdhubar and his strange death, he approaches
nearer the centaur Chiron, who was the companion
of Heracles. By his name he was the son of Hea,
whom Berosus identifies as Cronos, as Chiron was
the son of Cronos. Like Chiron, he was celebrated
for his wisdom, and acted as the counsellor of the
hero, interpreting his dreams, and enabling him to
overcome the enemies who attacked him. Chiron
met his death at the hand of Heracles, one of whose

poisoned arrows struck him, and, though immortal, would not live any longer, and gave his immortality to Prometheus. On this last statement I shall have something rather important to say later on. Zeus made Chiron among the stars a Saggitarius. Here again we have a striking echo of the Chaldean legend in the Erech story. According to the arrangement of tablets, the death of Hea-bani takes place under the sign of Saggitarius, and is the result of some fatal accident during the combat between Gizdhubar and Khumbaba. Like the centaurs before his call to the court of Gizdhubar, Hea-bani led a wild and savage life. It is said on the tablets " that he consorted with the wild beasts. With the gazalles he took his food by night, and consorted with the cattle by day, and rejoiced his heart with the creeping things of the waters." Dean Stanley made the very wise remark, in one of his lectures on the Jewish Church, that Nebuchadnezzar the Great became with the Chaldeans and later Jews a second Nimrod. Have we here, then, the origin of the story of Nebuchadnezzar's madness?

The third book of the Epic corresponds to the months of the Twins, the sign of Gemini; and we have the appropriate story of the twin sisters Samkhat and Kharimat, the beautiful females, who are sent to entice Hea-bani to Erech. These two creatures are the handmaids of Istar, the goddess of Erech. Their names indicate them to be personifications of pleasure and lust.   As Dp. Sam-kha-a-ti is derived from the root שׂמח, and corresponds to the Hebrew שִׂמְחָה, joy or pleasure ; and her companion, Kha-ri-ma-ti, from the root חרם, means the "devotee," and is equivalent in meaning to the Hebrew קְדֵשָׁה, "the women consecrated to the temple of Venus," who are also called Kadistuv in the inscriptions.   To the persuasive words of the one, and the loving actions of the other, the sage, like St Anthony, yields, and the tablet says—"At the words of her mouth, his wisdom fled away."   He consented to come to the court of Gizdhubar at Erech.   In order to test the struggle of the hero, he brings with him the Mirdarm, which Mr Houghton thinks to be a tiger, but which, I expect, is another name for the lion, and forms possibly the subject of the fifth story, corresponding to the sign Leo.   Mr Smith, who never could be brought to see the mythological character of Gizdhubar, and always regarded him as a king of Babylon, and was still more stubborn on the subject of the arrangement according to the zodiac, made his fourth and fifth books of the Epic to contain an account of the war between Gizdhubar and the Elamite giant Khumbaba, who is called " the strong one who dwells in the dark land of the pine tree," and " whose weapon was the tempest, which he poured forth from his mouth, and he took in his hand the Pierce, at which all men quake."   It is evident to me that these fragments do not come in here, but rather under the month, "the cloudy month," of the Akkadians—the month Kislen, or "the giant" of the Semites, and sign of Saggitarius. It was the month of November, the month of the months of thunder, storms, and rain. And Khumbaba, whose name appears to mean "the maker of darkness," poured forth storm from his mouth, and was armed with piercers, at which all men quake. We may safely therefore identify this mythic by the storm and thundercloud, armed with the lightning, which came sweeping from the mountains of the East, the land of Elam, over the plains. Khumbaba being called an Elamite, here indicates that, at the time when this Epic was compiled, the old nature myths were becoming Ethnic myths, and the war in heaven becoming the national wars of Babylon against her neighbours. We have several traces of this in the Hebrew writing, such as Shamgar, who slew 600 Philistines with an oxgoad; Gideon, the hewer-down; and most of all in the Hebrew Heracles Samson, whose deeds have many parallels in the story of Gizdhubar. Another fact that seems to support this transposition is, that the regent of the month is "Nergal, the War god," and who is called "the mighty hero of the gods;" and Merodach, as the star of Babylon, is called Alam, "the shadow," as if referring to the clouds. I shall not therefore, in the face of the mutilated condition of the fragments, attempt to restore in any way the fourth and

F

fifth books. In the month Elul or Ulul of the Semites—the "monthly message of the goddess" of the Akkadians, corresponding to our August—the sun had reached the zenith of his power—a time when in Palestine the heat is intense. So now we find Gizdhubar at the zenith of his power when he attracts the eyes of the lustful queen of heaven, the goddess Istar; so in the Sixth Tablet corresponding to the sign of Virgo, we have the story of the proposal of Istar to Gizdhubar. This tablet is fortunately in very good preservation, so one can give some fuller details showing the construction of the Epic. The hero having put on his crown, the goddess thus addressed him :—

(For the favour of Gizdhubar, the Princess Istar lifted up her eyes) :—
" Kiss me, Gizdhubar, that I may marry thee ;
Thy word to me as a bond place also ?
Thou, then, shalt husband me, and I then will wife thee ;
Thou shalt ride in a chariot of crystal and gold,
Of which the body is silver, and splendid its pole.
Thou shalt yoke daily, daily strong mules.
To our house in its fragrance the cedar spreads
To our house at thy entrance.
The Euphrates shall kiss thy feet.
(They shall place) below thee all kings, lords, and princes.
Gifts from mountain and plain they shall bring thee as taxes.
(Thy herds), and flocks of many sheep shall bring forth twins.
The race, thy mules shall be swift.
(Bearing) thee in thy 　　　　　　　, may they be strong and not weak.
And, in the yoke, equals they have not."

The value of this passage consists in the idea it gives of the position of the ancient chieftain, almost Homeric in character, his income being derived from dues and taxes. There is a bilingual hymn, Assyrian and Akkadian, which gives almost the same words as this, showing how there were royal titles in kind on all objects. Honey and milk flow in the land. The mountain brings tribute, the plain brings tribute, the fruit-garden brings tribute to the princely king of the land, who has on his right hand the sun, on his left hand the moon (W. A. I., vol. IV., pl. 18, No. 3). The hero knows, however, the danger of yielding to the love charms of this fickle queen, and tells her that corpses and carrion, disease, and famine form the emblems of her divinity and the insignia of her royalty. He then relates to her with bitter sarcasm her former amours, and here we have preserved a series of minor legends which the compiler of the poem has woven into the Epic. The first referred to is Tammuz Adonis. "For Tammuz (Adonis) thy husband, who year by year bewails his enchantment." The association of Tammuz, or Dunuzi, as he is called, the deification of the young summer sun, is brought on in several other passages in the inscriptions. In one hymn (W. A. I., IV., pl. xxvii., No. 1) we read— "The princely Lord Tammuz, the husband of Istar." The epithet here, *ucuv bcliv* (princely lord), reminds us of the Phœnician title *Adonai*, "the lord." The celebration of the annual festival of the marriage of

Istar and Tammuz, and the mourning for Tammuz, took place at the summer solstice, and was one of the great festivals of the year, it having spread to Phœnicia, where the celebration took place in the beautiful glen of Aphaca, "the place of weeping," the modern Afka in the Lebanon; to Phrygia, where it assumed the form of the mourning for Atys; and it was one of the forms of idolatry practised in Jerusalem in the time of Ezekiel, where women wept for Tammuz in the north gate of Jerusalem, turning to that evil point where the cold boar's tusk of winter had slain the beloved youth. The colophon or rubric attached to that beautiful legend of the descent of Istar into the underworld, one of the most poetic of the Assyrian inscriptions, throws considerable light on the ceremonial 'of this festival. Here we find' Tammuz called "the youthful husband" of Istar and " my only brother," and the figures of the god and goddess were adorned with robes and jewels and placed on a bier, followed by a crowd of weeping men and women. The hero Gizdhubar now proceeds to enumerate the other loves of the goddess.

> Thou dost love Allal the eagle,
> Thou didst smite him and break his wings.
> He stood in the forest and begged for wings.
> Thou didst love a lion full of strength ;
> Seven times seven thou didst wound him.
> Thou didst love the horse glorious in war ;
> He bowed down . . . thou didst afflict him.
> Seven times without ceasing thou didst afflict him.
> To his mother Sillili, weeping, thou didst afflict him.

In these animal loves of the goddess we have probably stories based on the animals sacred to her. As goddess of war and the chase, both the horse and the lion would be sacred to her. In the story of the horse perhaps we have a reference to the story of the horse in the fable of the ox and the horse, of which I have spoken. We now come to human lovers.

> Thou didst love the shepherd Tabulu,
> Whom continually thou didst desire offerings.
> Each day he offered libations and victims.
> Thou didst strike him, and to a jackal thou didst turn
>   him.
> The people of his own village drove him out ;
> His dogs tore him to pieces.
> Thou didst love also Isullanu, the tiller of the soil,
> Who constantly his garden stuff brought thee.
> Each day he made bright thy dishes.
> In thy . . . thou didst bind him.
> My Isullanu, thy gathering we will eat,
> And wisely enjoy the goodness of thy pot herbs.
> Isullanu said to thee,
> As for me, why dost thou desire me ?
> Oh, mother ! without thou cookest I will not eat.
> *
> *
> *
> Thou heardest these things.
> Thou didst strike him, and into a pillar thou didst turn
>   him.
> Thou didst place him in the midst of a desert.
> And moreover many things I could add.
> And as for me, if thou lovest me, I like unto these will
>   become.

Here we have the goddess in the character of enchantress and mistress of witchcrafts, like Circe and Hecate. In this portion of the legend she exactly corresponds to the epithets applied to her, as the goddess of Nineveh, by the Hebrew prophet Nahum: "Because of the multitude of the whoredoms of the well-favoured harlot, the mistress of witchcrafts" (Nahum iii. 4). The goddess Hecate, it will be remembered, had a threefold character, sometimes being identified with Silene, in which she would correspond to Istar, as the goddess of the crescent moon; with Artemis, as the goddess of hunting, she would correspond to Istar, the archeress of the gods; and with Persephone, in which she may be compared to Istar descending into the underworld. In this tablet we have an early version of the Legend of Actaeon, which is strangely similar to that of Tabulu disowned by his own dogs; and the story of Isullanu resembles rather that of Circe. It is also interesting to notice here the manner in which Tabulu, the shepherd, and Isullanu, the tiller of the soil, are placed in opposition to one another, as we find Cain and Abel in the Hebrew legend of civilisation. The old feud between the herdsman and the agriculturist so common in ancient mythologies in the myths of civilisation presents itself here. Enraged at his reply, the goddess flees to heaven to the presence of her father Anu—the Chaldean Zeus—and her mother Anunitus, and there relates how Gizdhubar had scorned her, and begs for their divine aid in obtaining vengeance on the hero. To assist her, a winged bull, called the Bull of Heaven, is created, and sent to earth. Gizdhubar, however, aided by Hea-bani, slays the bull and enters in triumph into Erech. The goddess and her maids who fight against the hero remind us of Omphale and her amazons, or Cybele and the Corybantes. The goddess here appears in her character of *Bilat takhazi*, lady of battle, or sometimes "lady of war and conflict." This episode must be placed under the seventh month.

The eighth book is one of particular interest, as we have here a very close agreement between the Chaldean legends and those of the Grecian Heracles. These tablets relate to the wanderings of Gizdhubar in the desert to the west of Babylonia until he comes to a garden where the trees are covered with jewels as fruit. In this garden live two women, *Siduri* and *Sabitū*, with whom the hero converses. The region is guarded by two scorpion-men, of whom the inscription says, "Their crown was the threshold of heaven, and their footing in the underworld, and whose face burned with terribleness, and whose presence was death." It was their duty to guard the rising and setting sun. Here, then, we have a very striking parallel to the story of the journey of Heracles to the garden of the Hesperides. The women correspond to the Hesperides, while the scorpion-men are the representatives of Atlas, who assisted the hero to gather the apples. It is curious to note that one of the most favourite subjects of the Cypriote seal-engravers was the representation of this garden of the West. The scorpion-men here mentioned enable us to place this legend in its proper place under the sign of Scorpio.

Turning now to the calendar we find Kisleu. The sun has passed the summer solstice and the autumn equinox, and is now waning in power. As I have already said, under the month Kisleu I should place the story of the combat with Khumbaba to correspond to the month of clouds, the giant and the sign of Sagittarius. During the combat with Khumbaba the faithful companion of Gizdhubar, Hea-bani, the satyr, was slain. For we find the tenth tablet opening with the lamentations of the hero over his beloved companion—" Gizdhubar for Hea-bani his friend wept bitterly and lay on the ground." The bitter lamentations of the hero in the twelfth book lead me to think that in some measure, like Heracles, he was contributory to his companion's death. The hero is now afflicted with the terrible disease of leprosy, loses his hair and wanes in power, and yearns to know the secret of immortality. This he is told is only known to the translated sage *Shamas-napiste*, the sun of life, who had survived the Deluge, and had been taken away to dwell in an island at the mouths of the Tigris and Euphrates. This idea of the sick and weakened sun is common to many

mythologies.   We have a parallel to it in the illness
of Heracles produced by the poisoned robe of Nessus;
also in the loss of strength by Samson when shorn of
his hair.   To find his way to the Chaldean Noah he
has to take a guide, the Chaldean Charon, *Nis Hea*,
"the man of Hea," the boatman, who will pilot him
to the resting-place of the translated sage.   The god
Hea was the god of the rivers and seas, and one of
his titles was " the god of the boatmen."   This portion corresponds to the month Tabet, or rainy month
of the calendar,—The month of " the going forth on
the sea" of the Akkadian calendar.   They journey to
the island ; and in the eleventh tablet, corresponding
to the month of much rain and the month of destruction and the sign of Aquarius, we have the Deluge
legend woven into the Epic.

www.ingramcontent.com/pod-product-compliance
Lightning Source LLC
Chambersburg PA
CBHW031115020726
47495CB00007B/2205